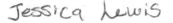
Jessica Lewis

P9-CCL-629

Christ Our Savior

"For unto you is born this day in the city of David a Saviour, which is Christ the Lord."

ELLEN WHITE
[Adapted.]

This is a faithful reproduction of the original

PUBLISHED BY THE
REVIEW AND HERALD PUBLISHING CO.
BATTLE CREEK, MICH.; CHICAGO, ILL.; ATLANTA, GA.

THE UPWARD WAY

P.O. Box 9009
Nampa, Id. 83652
Printed in the U.S.A.
by Pacific Press Publishing Association
Boise, Idaho

Pioneer Series
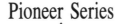

VOLUME 1

THE PIONEER SERIES

◆

I Christ, Our Savior
II Best Stories from the Best Book
III The Story of Joseph
IV Scrapbook Stories

ENTERED ACCORDING TO ACT OF
CONGRESS IN THE YEAR 1896, BY
MRS. E.G. WHITE
IN THE OFFICE OF THE LIBRARIAN
OF CONGRESS AT WASHINGTON,
D.C.

ART DIRECTION/COVER DESIGN ED GUTHERO
COVER ILLUSTRATION LARS JUSTINEN
NEW INSIDE PENCIL ILLUSTRATIONS DARREL TANK

The Upward Way
P.O. Box 9009 Nampa, Idaho 83652
ISBN 0-945460-05-8

*Upward Way For more information on this book
and other titles in the Pioneer Series call
1-800-FOR-BOOK.*

Dedication

To Tommy and all the other children of God who have been blessed by this story.

Preface.

❋

HE story of the earthly life of Christ our Saviour is written without words in ten thousand forms on every feature of nature, in every phase of human experience, in every fact of life. We never can fully realize how deep is the impression, how widespread is the influence of the life of Jesus of Nazareth. Every blessing of every kind comes to us through that connection between heaven and earth which was formed when the Lord of glory espoused the cause of a world lost in sin.

The infinite pathos of that story has inspired the pen of the learned and the tongue of the eloquent. But it is best told in child-like language. The wonderful spectacle needs no human coloring. Its glory surpasses the art of men. It shines brightest in its own luster.

In these pages no effort is made toward artificial embellishment. The plain story is simply told by a pen that is moved with a deep sense of the infinite proportions of the subject. The pen is controlled by a reverence for the sacred theme that preserves it unmarred by human suggestions, thus forming an appropriate sequel to the angelic announcement,—"Glory to God in the highest, and on earth peace, good will to men."

We are wont to sing in the familiar song—

"Tell me the story simply, as to a little child."

The author has done this. May it be received in the same simplicity and purity of faith. G. C. T.

Contents.

✻

Illustrations.

✻

THE CHILD JESUS AMONG THE DOCTORS.

" They found him in the temple, sitting in the midst of the doctors, both hearing them, and asking them questions."

His Mission.

BEFORE he came to this earth, Jesus was a great King in heaven. He was as great as God, and yet he loved the poor people of this earth so much that he was willing to lay aside his kingly crown, his beautiful robe, and come to this earth as one of the human family. We cannot understand how Christ became a little helpless babe. He could have come to earth in such beauty that he would have been unlike the sons of men. His face could have been bright with light, and his form could have been tall and beautiful.

He could have come in such a way as to charm those who looked upon him; but this was not the way that God planned he should come among the sons of men. He was to be like those who belonged to the human family and to the Jewish race. His features were to be like those of other human beings, and he was not to have such beauty of person as to make people point him out as different from others.

He was to come as one of the human family, and to stand as a man before heaven and earth. He had come to take man's place, to pledge himself in man's behalf, to pay the debt that sinners owed. He was to live a pure life on the earth, and show that Satan had told a falsehood when he claimed that the human family belonged to him forever, and that God could not take men out of his hands.

MEN first beheld Christ as a babe, as a child. His parents were very poor, and he had nothing in this earth save that which the poor have. He passed through all

the trials that the poor and lowly pass through from babyhood to childhood, from youth to manhood.

Nearly two thousand years ago a voice was heard in heaven from the throne of God, saying, "Sacrifice and offering thou didst not desire; mine ears hast thou opened; burnt offering and sin offering thou hast not required. Then said I, Lo, I come: in the volume of the book it is written of me, I delight to do thy will, O my God: yea, thy law is within my heart."

The more we think about Christ becoming a babe here on earth, the more wonderful it appears. How can it be that the helpless babe in Bethlehem's manger is still the divine Son of God? Though we cannot understand it, yet we can believe that he who made the worlds, for our sake became a helpless babe.

Though higher than any of the angels, though as great as the Father on the throne of heaven, yet he became one with us. In him God and man became one, and it is in this fact that we find the hope of our fallen race. Looking upon Christ in the flesh, we look upon God in humanity, and see in him the brightness of divine glory, the express image of God the Father.

From his earliest years, Christ lived a life of toil. In his youth he worked with his father at the carpenter's trade, and thus showed that there is nothing of which to be ashamed in work. Though he was the King of heaven, yet he worked at a humble trade, and thus rebuked all idleness in human beings. All work done as Christ did his work is noble and honorable. Those who are idle do not follow the example that Christ has given;

ANGEL and SHEPHERDS

for from his childhood he was a pattern of obedience and industry.

He was as a pleasant sunbeam in the home circle. Faithfully and cheerfully he acted his part, doing the humble duties that he was called to do in his lowly life. Christ became one with us in order that he might do us good. He lived such a life of poverty and labor as would help the poor to understand that he could sympathize with them. He himself shared the burdens of the lowly. The King of glory lived a life of toil.

The world's Redeemer did not live a life of selfish ease and pleasure. He did not choose to be the son of a rich man, or to be in a position where men would praise and flatter him. He passed through the hardships of those who toil for a living, and he could comfort all those who have to work at some humble trade.

The story of his life of toil is written so that we may receive comfort out of it. Those who know the kind of life Christ lived, can never feel that the poor are to be despised, and that those who are rich are better than the humble.

It is written of Jesus in his childhood, "The child grew, and waxed strong in spirit, filled with wisdom; and the grace of God was upon him." Every year his parents went to the city of Jerusalem to attend the feast of the Passover, and in his twelfth year Jesus went with them to the city.

When the feast was over, the parents, forgetting all about Jesus, started on their road home with some of their relatives, and did not know that Jesus was not with them. They supposed that he was in the company, and went a

whole day's journey before they found out that he was not there. Frightened as to what had become of him, they turned back to the city, and for three days they sought him with great anxiety.

"And it came to pass, that after three days, they found him in the temple, sitting in the midst of the doctors, both hearing them and asking them questions." The doctors were very learned men, and yet they were astonished as they heard Jesus ask wonderful questions, and saw that he had a good understanding of the Bible. His parents also listened in amazement, as they heard his searching questions.

Jesus knew that God had given him this opportunity to give light to those who were in darkness, and he sought to do all in his power to open the truth to the rabbis and teachers. He led these men to speak about different verses in the Bible that told about the Messiah whom they expected to come. They thought that Christ was to come to the world in great glory at this time, and make the Jewish nation the greatest nation on the earth. But Jesus asked them what the Scriptures meant when they spoke of the humble life, the suffering and sorrow, the rejection and death, of the Son of God.

Though Christ seemed like a child that was seeking help from those who knew a great deal more than he did, yet he was bringing light to their minds in every word he spoke. He repeated the scripture in such a way as gave them clear light in regard to the Lamb of God that taketh away the sins of the world. While he was teaching others, he himself was receiving light and knowledge about his own work and mission in the world; for it is plainly stated that Christ "grew in knowledge."

What a lesson there is in this for all the youth of our day. They may be like Christ, and by studying the word of God, by receiving the light that the Holy Spirit can give them, will be able to bring light to others. As they teach others of the grace of God, God will give them new grace from heaven. The more they try to teach others about the riches of Christ, the better understanding will they have of the plan of salvation, and the more richly will the grace of God abide in their own hearts. If the youth will remain as humble as did the child Jesus, they will become light-bearers to the world.

The wise men were surprised at the questions that the child Jesus asked. They wanted to encourage him in studying the Bible, and they wanted to see how much he knew about the prophecies. This is why they asked him so many questions. Joseph and Mary were as much surprised at the answers of their Son as were the wise men.

When there was a pause, Mary, the mother of Jesus, came up to her Son, and asked, "Son, why hast thou thus dealt with us? Behold, thy father and I have sought thee sorrowing." Then a divine light shone from Jesus' face as he lifted his hand, and said, "How is it that ye sought me? Wist ye not that I must be about my Father's business? And they understood not the saying which he spake unto them." They did not know what he really meant by these words, but they knew that he was a true son, who would be submissive to them. Though he was the Son of God, yet he went down to Nazareth, and was subject to his parents. Though his mother did not understand the meaning of his words, yet she did not forget them, but "kept all these sayings in her heart."

At the age of twelve, the people saw that the Holy Spirit was resting upon Jesus. He felt something of the burden of the mission for which he had come to our world. His soul was stirred into action. He helped them to understand the true meaning of the prophets, and showed them what the mission and work of the Messiah would be.

The Jewish people had wrong ideas about the Messiah and his work. They thought that when Christ came in their day, he would do grand and wonderful things, that he would set them above all other people. They were looking for the glory that will be seen when Christ comes the second time, and did not study the Bible so that they could know that he was to come the first time in a very lowly way. But Jesus asked questions about the scriptures that pointed to his first appearing, that flashed light into the minds of those willing to receive the truth.

Before he had come to the earth, he had given these prophecies to his servants, who had written them down, and now as he studied the Bible, the Holy Spirit brought these things to his mind, and showed him the great work that he was to do in the earth.

As he grew in knowledge, he imparted knowledge to others. But though he was wiser than the learned men, yet he did not become proud, or feel that he was above doing the most humble work. He took his share of the burden, with his father, mother, and brethren, and toiled to help support the family. Though the doctors had been amazed at his wisdom, yet he obeyed his parents, and worked with his own hands as any toiler would work. It is stated of Jesus that, as he grew older, "he increased in wisdom and stature, and in favor with God and man."

THE understanding that he obtained from day to day that showed him how wonderful should be his mission in the world, did not lead him to neglect the most humble duties. He cheerfully took up the work that children and youth who dwell in humble households are called upon to do; for he knew what it was to be pressed by poverty. He understands the temptations of children, for he bore their sorrows and trials.

Firm and steadfast was his purpose to do the right. Though others tried to lead him to do evil, yet he never did wrong, and would not turn away in the least from the path of truth and right. He always obeyed his parents, and did every duty that lay in his path. But his childhood and youth were not smooth and joyous. His spotless life aroused the envy and jealousy of his brothers. They were annoyed because he did not act in all things as they did, and would not become one with them in doing evil. In his home life he was cheerful, but never boisterous. He ever seemed like one who was seeking to learn. He took great delight in nature, and God was his teacher.

EVEN in his childhood Jesus saw that the people did not live in the way that the Bible pointed out they should live. He studied the Bible, and followed the simple habits and ways that the word of God directs, and when people found fault with him because he was so lowly and simple, he pointed them to the word of God.

His brothers told him that he thought himself much better than they were, and reproved him for setting himself up above the priests and rulers of the people. Jesus knew that if he obeyed the word of God, he would not

VISIT of the WISE MEN.

find rest and peace in the home circle among his brothers.

As he grew in knowledge, he knew that great errors were increasing among men, and that because the people followed the commands of men instead of obeying the commands of God, simplicity and truth and true piety were becoming lost in the earth. He saw the people going through forms and ceremonies in their worship of God, and passing by the sacred truths that made their service of value. He knew that their faithless services could not do them any good, and would not bring them peace or rest. They could not know what it was to have freedom of spirit when they did not serve God in truth.

Jesus did not always silently look upon these worthless services, but sometimes told the people where they were going wrong. Because he was so quick to see what was false and what was true, his brothers were greatly annoyed at him ; for they said that whatever the priests taught ought to be looked upon as sacred as a command of God. But Jesus taught both by his words and by his example that men ought to worship God just as he has directed them to, and not follow the ceremonies that men have said ought to be followed.

His brothers were greatly put out because Jesus would not do as their teachers directed, and followed the word of God rather than the traditions of men. The priests and the Pharisees also were annoyed because this child would not accept their human inventions, maxims, and traditions. They thought that he showed great disrespect to their religion and to the rabbis who had commanded these services. He told them that he would heed every word that came from the mouth of God, and that they must show him from the Bible where he was in error. He pointed out to them the fact that they were placing the word of men above the word of God, and causing men to show disrespect to God through obeying the commands of men.

THE rabbis knew that there was nothing in the Scriptures that would uphold them in forcing him to obey their traditions. They knew that he was far in advance of them in spiritual understanding, and that he lived a blameless life, yet they were angry with him because he would not violate his conscience by obeying their dictates. Failing to convince him that he ought to look upon human tradition as sacred, they came to Joseph and Mary, and complained that Jesus was taking a wrong course in regard to their customs and traditions.

Jesus knew what it was to have his family divided against him on account of his religious faith. He loved peace, he craved the love and confidence of the members of his family, but he knew what it was to have them withdraw their affections from him. He suffered rebuke and censure because he took a straightforward course, and would not do evil because others did evil, but was true to the commandments of Jehovah. His brothers rebuked him because he stood aloof from the ceremonies that were taught by the rabbis ; for they regarded the word of man more highly than the word of God, because they loved the praise of men more than the praise of God.

Jesus made the Scriptures his constant study, and when the scribes and Pharisees tried to make him do as they did, and accept their doctrines, they found him ready to meet them with the word of God, and could do nothing to convince him that they were right. He seemed to know the Scriptures from beginning to end, and repeated them in such a way that their true meaning shone out. They were ashamed because this child knew more than they did. They claimed that he ought to obey them, and not go contrary to the teachings of the church. They said it was their business to explain the Scriptures, and that it was his place to accept what they said. They were angry that this child should dare to question their word when it was their calling to study and explain the Scriptures.

The scribes, rabbis, and Pharisees could not force Jesus to turn from the word of God, and follow the traditions of men; but they could influence his brothers in such a way that his life might become a very bitter one. His brothers threatened him and sought to compel him to take a wrong course; but he passed on, making the Scriptures his guide.

From the time his parents found him in the temple, asking and answering questions among the doctors, they could not understand his course of action. Quiet and gentle, he seemed as one who was set apart. Whenever he could, he went out alone into the fields and on the mountainsides to commune with the God of nature. When his work was done, he wandered by the lakeside, among the trees of the forest, and in the green valleys, where he could think about God, and lift his soul to heaven in prayer.

After a season thus spent, he would return to his home to take up again the humble duties of his life, and to give to all an example of patient labor.

The Carpenter Shop of Nazareth

Jesus loved children, and ever influenced them for good. He cared for the poor and needy even in his childhood. In every gentle, tender, and submissive way, he sought to please those with whom he came in contact. But though so gentle and submissive, no one could lead him to do anything that was contrary to the word of God.

Some admired his perfection of character, and often sought to be with him. But others who regarded the sayings of men more than the word of God, turned away from him, and avoided his company. Throughout his childhood and youth he manifested the same perfection of character as marked his after life.

As Jesus looked upon the offerings that were brought as a sacrifice to the temple, the Holy Spirit taught him that his life was to be sacrificed for the life of the world. He grew up as a tender plant, not in a large and noisy city, full of confusion and strife, but in the retired valleys and among the hills.

From his earliest years he was guarded by heavenly angels, yet his life was one long struggle against the powers of darkness. Satan sought in every way to tempt and try him. He caused men to misunderstand his words, so that they might not receive the salvation he came to bring them. He was opposed both at home and abroad, not because he was an evil-doer, but because his life was free from every taint of sin, and condemned all impurity.

He found his greatest happiness in communing with nature and with nature's God. He was faithful in obeying the commands of God, and this made him very different from those who were around him who disregarded the word of God. His stainless life was a rebuke, and many avoided his presence. But there were some who sought to be with him because they felt at peace where he was, he was so gentle, and never contended for his rights.

His own brothers scorned and hated him, showing that they did not believe in him, and casting contempt upon him. In his home life, where he should have found peace, he found strife, envy, and jealousy. He loved his brothers, but they made his labors unnecessarily hard because he was so willing and uncomplaining. He did not fail nor become discouraged. He lived above the difficulties of his life, as if in the light of God's countenance. He bore insult patiently, and in his human nature became an example for all children and youth.

CHRIST showed the greatest respect and love for his mother. Though she often talked with him and sought to have him do as his brothers desired him to do, yet he never showed her the least lack of devotion. His brothers could not cause him to change his habits of life. He knew there was nothing wrong in thinking about the works of God, in showing sympathy and tenderness toward the poor, the suffering, and the unfortunate. He sought to soothe the sufferings of both men and dumb animals.

Mary had felt greatly troubled when the rabbis came to her to complain about Jesus, but peace and confidence came to her troubled heart as her Son showed her what the Scriptures said about his practices. At times she wavered between Jesus and his brothers who did not believe that he was the Sent of God; but she saw enough to show her that his was a divine character. She saw

him giving his life for others, meeting the people where they were. She saw him growing in grace and knowledge, and in favor with God and man.

His life was as leaven, working amid the elements of society. Harmless and undefiled he walked amid the careless, the thoughtless, the rude and unholy. He mingled with the unjust publicans, the reckless prodigals, the unrighteous Samaritans, the heathen soldiers, the rough peasants, and the mixed multitudes. He looked upon them all with pity and love. He addressed himself to them, not for the purpose of discouraging and condemning them, but to present lessons to them that would be a savor of life unto life to those who should believe.

He treated every human being as having great value. He taught men to look upon themselves as persons to whom had been given precious talents, that if rightly used, would elevate and ennoble them, and secure for them eternal riches.

By his example and character he taught that every moment of life was precious, as a time in which to sow seed for eternity. From childhood to manhood, he worked out in his life the principle of the law of God. He weeded life of all vanities, and taught that it was to be cherished as a treasure, and be employed for holy purposes.

He taught that the character was precious, and that every moment of life was to be passed in the service of God in such a way as to be a saving salt to preserve society from moral corruption. Christ passed no human being by as worthless and hopeless, but sought to apply the saving remedy to every soul who needed help.

WHEREVER he was found, he had a lesson to present that was the right one for the time and circumstance. He sought to inspire with hope the most rough and unpromising, setting before them the idea that they might become blameless and harmless, and attain a character that would be Christlike. They could be the children of God, even though they lived among evil people, and could shine as lights in the world. This was the reason that so many heard him gladly. From his very childhood he worked for others, letting his light shine amid the moral darkness of the world. In bearing burdens in his home life, and in laboring in more public fields, he showed men what the character of God is. He encouraged everything that had a bearing on the real interests of life; but he did not encourage the youth in dreaming of what would be in the future. He taught them by his words and by his example that the future would be decided by the way in which they spent the present.

Our destiny is marked out by our own course of action. Those who cherish that which is right, who work out God's plan, it may be in a narrow sphere of action, who do right because it is right, will find wider fields of usefulness. Those who are true to God's holy commandments in a humble place, are fitting themselves to do service in some higher position. The Lord will bless them with views of eternity, will help them to purify and elevate their character. They may be as conscious of the favor of God as was Christ.

———

THE Jews thought themselves better than other people, and held themselves aloof from other nations; but Jesus mingled with all classes of people. He had come to seek and to save that which was lost.

The brothers of Christ were angry because he did not feel the same prejudice against the poor and the outcast as they did. They did not understand Jesus.

Through childhood, youth, and manhood, Christ walked alone. In his purity, in his faithfulness, he trod the wine-press alone, and of the people there was none with him. It is our privilege now to act a part in the work and mission of Christ. We may be laborers together with him. In whatever work we are called to engage, we may work with Christ. He is doing all that he can to set us free, to make our lives, that seem so cramped and narrow, reach out to bless and help others.

He would have us understand that we are responsible to do good, and to realize that in shunning our work we are bringing loss upon ourselves. In his day he saw many that were falling far below what they might be in becoming useful. To those who were doing nothing, he said, "Why stand ye here all the day idle?" We are to work while it is called day; for the night cometh, in which no man can work.

Jesus carried the burden of the salvation of the human family upon his heart. He knew that unless men would receive him, and become changed in purpose and life, they would be eternally lost. This was the burden of his soul, and he was alone in carrying this load. No one knew how heavy was the weight that rested upon his heart. But from his youth he was filled with a deep longing to be a lamp in the world, and he purposed that his life should be "the light of the world."

ANGELS APPEARING TO THE SHEPHERDS.

"Behold, I bring you good tidings of great joy."

The Birth of Jesus.

N the little town of Nazareth, nestled among the hills of northern Galilee, was the home of Joseph and Mary, who were afterward known as the earthly parents of Jesus.

Now Joseph was of the lineage, or family, of David; and so, when a decree was sent out for the taxing of the nation, he had to go to Bethlehem, the city of David, to have his name enrolled.

This was a toilsome journey, in the way people had to travel in those times, and Mary, who accompanied her husband, was very weary as they climbed the hill on which Bethlehem stands.

How she longed for a comfortable place to rest! But the inns were already full, and while the rich and proud were well cared for, this humble pair had to seek shelter in a rude building where cattle were fed.

They were not poor; for though they had few earthly possessions, God loved them, and that gave contentment and peace. They were children of the Heavenly King, who was about to honor them above all earthly beings.

Angels had been watching them while they were on their journey, and as they went to rest in their humble lodgings, they were not alone: angels were still with them.

THE JOURNEY TO BETHLEHEM.

It was here, in this lowly shed, that Jesus, our Saviour, was born and laid in a manger. In this rude cradle lay the Son of the Highest,—he whose presence had lately filled the courts of heaven with glory.

There, he had been adored by angels; here, the beasts of the stall were his companions. But the place could not dishonor him; he gave it a glory that will not depart from it so long as the name of Bethlehem is known.

The priests and great ones among the Jews were not ready to welcome the birth of the Saviour. They had not longed for his appearing, and were too proud to believe that this babe in the manger could be the coming Messiah.

So God sent bright messengers from his own throne of light to tell the glad news to some humble shepherds, — godly men, who were keeping watch over their flocks by night on the plains of Bethlehem.

These devoted shepherds were thinking about the promise of a Messiah, and waiting for his coming. To these, the heavenly message could be revealed. They could appreciate and welcome it.

"And, lo, the angel of the Lord came upon them, and the glory of the Lord shone round about them : and they were sore afraid. And the angel said unto them, Fear not : for, behold, I bring you good tidings of great joy, which shall be to all people. For unto you is born this day in the city of David a Saviour, which is Christ the Lord.

"And this shall be a sign unto you ; Ye shall find the babe wrapped in swaddling clothes, lying in a manger. And suddenly there was with the angel a multitude of the heavenly host praising God, and saying, Glory to God in the highest, and on earth peace, good will toward men.

"And it came to pass, as the angels were gone
away from them into heaven, the shepherds said one
to another, Let us now go even unto Bethlehem, and
see this thing which is come to pass, which the Lord
hath made known unto us.

"And they came with

VISIT OF THE SHEPHERDS.

haste, and found Mary, and Joseph, and the babe lying in the manger. And when they had seen it,
they made known abroad the saying which was told
them concerning this child.

"And all they that heard it wondered at those things
which were told them by the shepherds. But Mary
kept all these things, and pondered them in her
heart."[1]

[1] Luke 2 : 9–19.

Jesus Presented in the Temple.

JOSEPH and Mary were Jews, and followed the customs of their nation. When the infant Jesus was eight days old, he was circumcised, according to the commandment given to Abraham.[1] In this, God would have an example of obedience set by his own Son, the Prince of heaven.

At one time the Children of Israel dwelt in Egypt for many years. When the Egyptians had grown cruel to them, and tried to make them slaves, God raised up Moses to set them free.

The king of Egypt refused to let the Israelites go ; so God sent fearful plagues upon the Egyptians. The last of these plagues was the slaying of the first-born in every house, from the palace of the king to the lowliest dwelling in the land.

The Lord told Moses that every family of the Israelites must kill a lamb, and put some of the blood upon the door-posts of their dwelling. This

[1] Gen. 17 : 12.   [29]

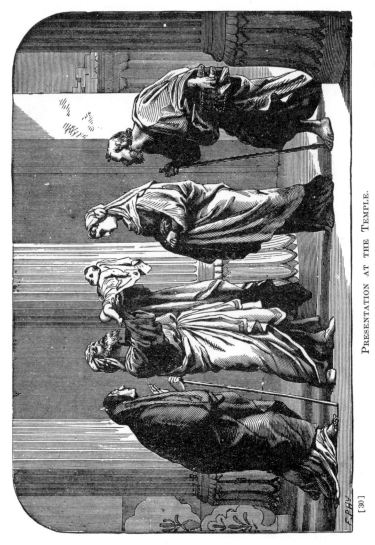

Presentation at the Temple.

"Now lettest thou thy servant depart in peace, for mine eyes have seen thy salvation."

[30]

was so that the angel of death might *pass over* all the houses of the Israelites, and destroy none but the proud Egyptians.

This blood of the " passover " represented to the Jews the blood of the world's Redeemer.

STRIKING THE DOOR-POST

THE PASSOVER SUPPER

DEATH OF THE FIRSTBORN

For, in due time, God would give his dear Son to be slain as the lamb had been slain ; so that all who should believe in him might be saved from ever-lasting death. Christ is called our passover. 1 Corinthians 5 : 7. He was " slain from the foundation of the world." Revelation 13 : 8. By his blood we are redeemed. Ephesians 1 : 7.

In remembrance of this great deliverance from death by the plague, and to keep in mind the greater deliverance to be wrought out by the Son of God, every first-born man-child was to be presented to the Lord in the temple. So when Jesus was six weeks old, Joseph and Mary took him to the priest, and made the offering required by the law.

In the persons of Joseph and Mary, the priest saw nothing remarkable. They were simple working people from Galilee. In the child Jesus he saw merely a helpless infant. Little did the priest think that he was holding in his hands the Saviour of the world, the high priest of the heavenly sanctuary. But he might have known; for if he had been such a man as he ought to have been, God would have shown him these things.

There were in the temple at this very time two of God's true servants. They had both grown old in the service of their heavenly Master, and he intrusted to them things that he had to withhold from the proud and worldly-minded priests.

Simeon had the promise that he should not die till he had seen the Messiah. As soon as he saw Jesus in the temple, he knew him to be the Anointed of the Lord. Taking the child in his arms, he blessed God, and said,—

"Lord, now let thy servant depart in peace, according to thy word; for mine eyes have seen thy salvation, which thou hast prepared before the face of all people,— a light to lighten the Gentiles, and the glory of thy people Israel." [2]

Anna, the prophetess, was a woman of great age. She "served God with fastings and prayers night and day.

"And she, coming in that instant, gave thanks likewise unto the Lord, and spake of him to all them that looked for redemption in Jerusalem." [3]

So it is that God chooses humble people for his witnesses. Those that the world calls great are not often called to bear the light of truth and mercy to those who have lost their way in the dark paths of sin.

Mary, the mother of Jesus, could hardly believe that the Lord was to give her such great honor. In her joy and surprise she said, "My soul doth magnify the Lord." "For he that is mighty hath done to me great things ; and holy is his name."

"He hath put down the mighty from their seats, and exalted them of low degree. He hath filled the hungry with good things ; and the rich he hath sent empty away." [4]

[2] Luke 2 : 29–32.　　　　　　　　　[3] Luke 2 : 38.
[4] Luke 1 : 46, 49, 52, 53.

[34]

JOURNEY OF THE WISE MEN.

"We have seen his star in the east, and have come to worship him."

The Visit of the Wise Men.

GOD would not leave the people ignorant concerning the mission of his Son. The priests, who ought to have been faithful teachers of divine things, were in darkness themselves. They could not recognize the Messiah; but God sent angels to tell the shepherds that Christ was born, and where they might find him.

So, too, when Jesus was presented in the temple, God had his witnesses ready. He had preserved their lives till they had the joyful privilege of testifying that the infant Jesus was the very Christ,—the Anointed One.

God meant that others, as well as the Jews, should know that the Saviour had come, to begin his earthly mission. In the far East were wise men who had read the prophecies concerning the coming Messiah, and believed that he would soon appear.

The Jews looked upon these men as heathen philosophers merely. But these philosophers were not

3   [35]

idolaters. They were honest men, anxious to know the truth, and the mind of God.

God looks upon the heart, and he knew that these men could be trusted. They were in a better condition to receive light from heaven than were the haughty priests, so

THE NEW STAR.

steeped in selfishness, and so encased in pride.

These wise men had traced the handiwork of God in nature, and learned to love him there. They had studied the stars, and knew their movements. They were familiar with the nightly march of the heavenly bodies. If a star were missing, they would know it. If a new one should appear, they would hail it as a great event.

These men had noticed in the sky the strange light caused by the glory that surrounded the host of angels when they visited the shepherds on the plains of Bethlehem.

When this light faded away, they had seen what appeared to be a new star in the heavens. They thought at once of the prophecy which says, "There shall come a star out of Jacob, and a scepter shall rise out of Israel."[1]

Had this star come to tell them that Messiah had appeared? They would follow it, and see what it would lead to. It led them into Judea; but when they came nigh to Jerusalem, the star grew dim, and they could not follow it.

Supposing that the Jews could at once direct them to the infant Saviour, the wise men went into the city of Jerusalem, and said,—

"Where is he that is born King of the Jews? for we have seen his star in the east, and are come to worship him."

"When Herod the king had heard these things, he was troubled, and all Jerusalem with him. And when he had gathered all the chief priests and scribes of the people together, he demanded of them where Christ should be born. And they said unto him, In Bethlehem of Judea; for thus it is written by the prophet."

But Herod was much disturbed. He did not like

[1] Numbers 24 : 17.

to hear of a king of the Jews who might take his place in ruling the nation. So he had a private talk with the wise men, enquiring of them " diligently what time the star appeared."

Then he sent them to Bethlehem, and said, " Go, and search diligently for the young child ; and when ye have found him, bring me word again, that I may come and worship him also."

When the wise men heard what the king had to say, they took up their journey again ; "And, lo, the star, which had been seen in the east, went before them, till it came and stood over where the young child was." When they saw the star again, they were encouraged, and " rejoiced with exceeding great joy."

When they had come into the house over which the star rested, " They saw the young child with Mary his mother, and fell down and worshiped him : and when they had opened their treasures, they presented unto him gifts,— gold, and frankincense, and myrrh." [2]

How readily these wise men accepted the infant Jesus as the one they had come so far to find. They believed the sign that had been given them ; and as they worshiped, and poured out their treasures, they had no doubt that the Saviour of the world was before them.

[2] Mattbew 2

From Childhood To Manhood.

HEROD was not honest when he said he wanted to come and worship Jesus. He feared that the Saviour would grow up to be a king, and take his kingdom from him. He wanted to know where he could find the child, so that he might have him put to death.

The wise men prepared to return and tell Herod. But the angel of the Lord appeared to them in a dream and sent them home another way.

"And when they were departed, behold, the angel of the Lord appeareth to Joseph in a dream, saying, Arise, and take the young child and his mother, and flee into Egypt, and be thou there until I bring thee word; for Herod will seek the young child to destroy him."[1]

Joseph did not wait till morning, but arose at once and started by night on his long journey. The wise

[1] Matthew 2: 13.   [39]

THE JOURNEY TO EGYPT.

"Take the young child and his mother, and flee into Egypt."

men had given costly presents to Jesus, and in this way God provided for the expenses of the journey and their stay in Egypt, until they should return to their own land.

Herod was very angry when he found that the wise men had gone home another way. In his wrath he sent soldiers to kill " all the children that were in Bethlehem, . . . from two years old and under, according to the time which he had diligently inquired of the wise men."

How strange that a man should fight against God! What an awful scene this slaying of the innocent children must have been! Herod had done many cruel things before, and God allowed him to do this also; but he did not live to do many more wicked deeds; for he soon died a sudden and terrible death.

Joseph and Mary remained in Egypt till after the death of Herod. Then the angel appeared to Joseph, and said, "Arise, and take the young child and his mother, and go into the land of Israel; for they are dead which sought the young child's life."[2]

On coming near to Judea, he learned that a son of Herod was reigning in place of his father. This made Joseph afraid to go there, and he did not know what to do; but God sent an angel to instruct him.

Following the directions of the angel, Joseph returned to his old home in Nazareth. Here Jesus

[2] Matthew 2 : 16, 20.

remained with Joseph and Mary till he was nearly thirty years old, and was "subject unto them."

In the humble carpenter shop, and wherever his labor called him, the youthful Jesus worked for wages, and thus aided in the support of the family.

The time had come for

THE CARPENTER SHOP AT NAZARETH.

Jesus to begin his ministry. His first act was to go to the Jordan and be baptized by John the Baptist.

John was sent to prepare the way for the Saviour. While he was preaching in the wilderness, God made known to him that some day the Messiah would come to him and ask to be baptized. He was also told that a sign would be given him, that he might know certainly who it was.

When Jesus came, John recognized in his face such signs of his holy life that he forbade him, saying : —

" I have need to be baptized of thee, and comest thou to me ? "

" And Jesus answering said unto him, Suffer it to be so now ; for thus it becometh us to fulfil all righteousness." [3]

So John led the Saviour down into the waters of the beautiful Jordan. And there he baptized him in the sight of all the people.

Jesus was not baptized to show repentance for his own sins, for he had never sinned. He did it for sinful men, and to set an example for them to follow.

When he came up out of the water, he kneeled down on the bank of the river, and prayed earnestly to God. And his Father heard that prayer ; for the heavens were opened, and beams of glory streamed forth, " and he saw the Spirit of God descending like a dove, and lighting upon him." His face and form were all aglow with the light of the glory of God.

And from heaven the voice of God was heard saying : —

"This is my beloved Son, in whom I am well pleased." [4]

This scene beside the Jordan was one of the most wonderful events that has ever taken place between heaven and earth. It was full of meaning for sinful man. The glory that rested on Christ was a pledge of the love of God to man.

[3] Matthew 3 : 14, 15.   [4] Matthew 3 : 16, 17.

The Temptation.

He was led by the Spirit into the wilderness.

FTER the baptism of Jesus, he was led by the Spirit into the wilderness, to be tempted of the devil.

As he left the Jordan, his face was lighted with the glory which had surrounded him there. But as he neared the wilderness, this glory departed. The sins of the world were pressed upon him, and his face showed such sorrow and anguish as man had never felt. He was suffering for sinners.

Our first parents failed on the point of appetite. It was this which led them to disobey God, and brought sin and sorrow and death into the world. Christ began where Adam fell. He suffered the pangs of hunger for forty days, to show the race that appetite may be overcome.

The length of the fast endured by the Saviour is the strongest evidence of the sinfulness of debased appetite, and its power over the human family.

This terrible trial was not required because the Son of God needed the discipline. It was to teach mankind that every indulgence of appetite, bad habits, and passion must be conquered as Christ withstood the cravings of hunger during his long fast.

As soon as Christ began his fast, Satan appeared as an angel of light, and claimed to be a messenger from heaven.

If thou be the Son of God, command this stone that it be made bread.

He told him it was not the will of God that he should suffer this pain and self-denial. His Father had only wanted him to show his willingness to undergo it.

When Jesus was suffering the keenest pangs of hunger, Satan said to him : —

"If thou be the Son of God, command that these stones be made bread."

But the Saviour had to suffer as man suffers. Had he exercised his divine power and worked a miracle, it would have been contrary to his mission. His miracles were all for the good of others. He answered : —

"It is written, Man shall not live by bread alone, but by every word that proceedeth out of the mouth of God."

Thus Christ showed that the want of food is much less important than meeting the disfavor of God.

Failing in this temptation, the devil carried him to a pinnacle of the temple, and said to him : —

"If thou be the Son of God, cast thyself down ; for it is written, He shall give his angels charge concerning thee ; and in their hands they shall bear thee up, lest at any time thou dash thy foot against a stone."

Here Satan followed the example of Christ in quoting Scripture. But Jesus knew that this promise was not given to those who wilfully place themselves in the way of danger. Therefore he answered : —

"It is written again, Thou shalt not tempt the Lord thy God."

The sin of presumption lies close beside the line of perfect faith and trust. We must have childlike faith, and trust our heavenly Father ; but we must not presume on his mercy.

To refuse to obey any of God's requirements, and then claim that he is abundant in mercy, and will forgive, is presumption. God will forgive those who seek pardon and put away their transgression. But to continue in refusing to obey, and yet rely on God's mercy for pardon, is presuming upon his forgiveness.

Satan next took Jesus to the top of a high mountain, and showed him all the kingdoms of the world. The sunlight lay on templed cities, marble palaces, fruitful fields and vineyards, gilding the dark cedars of Lebanon and the blue waters of Galilee. And Satan said : —

"All these things will I give thee, if thou wilt fall down and worship me."

Jesus viewed the scene for only a moment, and then turned resolutely from it. He would not dally with the temptation by even looking at it. The love of the world, the lust for power, and the pride of life were all embraced in this temptation. Anything that draws mankind from the worship of the true God has its example in this last great trial of the Saviour.

"Then saith Jesus unto him, Get thee hence, Satan : for it is written, Thou shalt worship the Lord thy God, and him only shalt thou serve." [1]

The indignation of Christ was aroused, and he exercised his divine authority in the words, "Get thee hence." Satan had no power to withstand this command. He was obliged to go.

Writhing with baffled hate and rage, the rebel chief left the presence of the world's Redeemer. The contest was ended. Christ's victory was as complete as had been the failure of Adam.

[1] Matthew 4 : 3–10.

RETURN TO THE JORDAN.

"Behold the Lamb of God, which taketh away the sin of the world."

Early Ministry.

AFTER the temptation Jesus returned to the banks of the Jordan, and mingled with the disciples of John.

At that time men from the rulers at Jerusalem were questioning John as to his authority for teaching the people and baptizing. They asked if he was the Messiah, or Elias, or "that prophet" (referring to Moses). To all of which he answered, "I am not." They asked:—

"Who art thou? that we may give an answer to them that sent us?"

"He said, I am the voice of one crying in the wilderness, Make straight the way of the Lord, as said the prophet Esaias."[1]

At this moment John saw Jesus on the banks of the Jordan. His face lighted up as he pointed to him and said:—

"There standeth one among you, whom ye know not; he it is, who coming after me is preferred before

[1] John 1 : 22, 23; Isaiah 40 : 3.

me, whose shoe's latchet I am not worthy to unloose." [2]

The next day John again saw Jesus, and cried:—
"Behold the Lamb of God, which taketh away the sin of the world!"

Two of the disciples of John hearing this, followed the Saviour.   Other disciples were chosen as they journeyed on their way to Galilee.

At the marriage in Cana

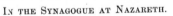
In the Synagogue at Nazareth.

of Galilee he performed the wonderful miracle of turning water into wine. This act was a symbol of the means of salvation. The water typified baptism, and the wine the blood of Christ.

Jesus went to his old home at Nazareth, and entered a synagogue on the Sabbath.   He here proclaimed his mission to the world.   But his hearers remembered his humble birth, and that he was only a carpenter. This led them to reject their Saviour, and they thus lost the blessing that had come to them.

[2] John 1: 26, 27.

Teachings of Jesus.

"Stretch forth thine hand"

THE religion of the Jews had become little more than a round of ceremonies. As they lost sight of the true worship of God and the spiritual power of his word, they had added ceremonies and traditions of their own to take their place.

Instead of realizing that only the blood of the coming Saviour could cleanse them from sin, and that the power of God alone could keep them from its power, they relied on their own works and the ceremonies of their religion to earn them salvation.

The scribes, Pharisees, and rulers had become a self-righteous class. Jesus knowing their true condition, rebuked them many times. He at one time described them in the following words:—

"Woe unto you, scribes and Pharisees, hypocrites! for ye are like unto whited sepulchers, which indeed appear beautiful outward, but are within full of dead men's bones, and of all uncleanness. Even so ye also

THE DISCIPLES PLUCKING CORN.

"Behold, thy disciples do that which is not lawful to do upon the Sabbath day."

outwardly appear righteous unto men, but within ye are full of hypocrisy and iniquity."[1]

The Saviour came to restore the true worship of God, and strip from it the burdensome traditions which had been built around it. He came to bring in a pure, heart religion, that would manifest itself in a pure life and a holy character.

In the beautiful sermon on the mount he pronounced special blessings on the " poor in spirit," the ones that " mourn," the " meek," those who " hunger and thirst after righteousness," the " merciful," the " pure in heart," the " peacemakers," and those who are " persecuted " and " reviled " for righteousness' sake.[2]

This kind of religion found no favor with the self-righteous rulers of Israel. And as they saw the deep interest attending the work of Christ, they became alarmed. Their false theories and works were being shown to the people, and they were losing influence. So they used every means at their command to hinder the Saviour in his work.

One Sabbath day, as Jesus and his disciples were passing through a field of grain, the disciples broke off some of the heads, rubbed them in their hands, and ate the kernels, for they were hungry. But spies were always on his track. They were watching for some occasion to accuse and condemn him. When

[1] Matthew 23 : 27, 28.   [2] Matthew 5 : 1-12.

they saw what the disciples were doing, they said to the Saviour : —

"Behold, thy disciples do that which is not lawful to do upon the Sabbath day."[3]

But Jesus defended his followers. He reminded their accusers of David, who, when in need, had eaten of the sacred bread of the tabernacle, and given it to his hungry followers. If David might do this without blame, might not the disciples pluck the grain necessary to supply the demands of hunger?

The Sabbath was not made to be a burden to man. It was to give him peace and rest, and to remind him of the work of his Creator. It was to be a delight; therefore our Lord said, "The Sabbath was made for man, and not man for the Sabbath."[4]

"And it came to pass also on another Sabbath, that he entered into the synagogue and taught; and there was a man whose right hand was withered.

"And the scribes and Pharisees watched him, whether he would heal on the Sabbath day; that they might find an accusation against him.

"But he knew their thoughts, and said to the man which had the withered hand, Rise up, and stand forth in the midst. And he arose and stood forth.

"Then said Jesus unto them, I will ask you one thing: Is it lawful on the Sabbath days to do good, or to do evil? to save life, or to destroy it?

[3] Matthew 12:2.　　　　[4] Mark 2:27.

"And looking round about upon them all, he said unto the man, Stretch forth thy hand. And he did so; and his hand was restored whole as the other.

"And they were filled with madness; and communed one with another what they might do to Jesus."[5]

Jesus showed them how unreasonable they were by asking them a question. "And he said unto them, What man shall there be among you, that shall have one sheep, and if it fall into a pit on the Sabbath day, will he not lay hold on it, and lift it out?"

This they could not answer. So he said, "How much then is a man better than a sheep? Wherefore it is lawful to do well on the Sabbath days."[6]

"It is lawful." That is, it is according to law. Jesus never reproved the Jews for reverencing the law of God, or for keeping the Sabbath. On the contrary, he ever upheld the law in all its completeness.

Isaiah prophesied of Christ, "He will magnify the law, and make it honorable."[7] To magnify is to make larger and broader, to raise to a higher position.

To those who claim that Jesus came to abolish the law, he said, "Think not that I am come to destroy the law, or the prophets; I am not come to destroy, but to fulfil." To fulfil means to keep. See James 2 : 8.

God's law can never be changed, for Christ said, "Till heaven and earth pass, one jot or one tittle shall in no wise pass from the law, till all be fulfilled."[8]

[5] Luke 6 : 6–11.
[7] Isaiah 42 : 21.
[6] Matthew 12 : 11, 12.
[8] Matthew 5 : 17, 18.

In the examples given by Christ, he endeavored to sweep away their false ideas, by making the Sabbath more honorable than before. This lesson teaches that it is the highest type of Sabbath-keeping to engage in acts of mercy toward the suffering on that day.

When Jesus asked the question, "Is it lawful on the Sabbath days to do good, or to do evil? to save life, or to destroy it?" he showed that he could read the hearts of the wicked Pharisees who accused him. He knew that, while he was trying to save life, they were hunting his life with bitter hatred. Was it better to slay upon the Sabbath, as they were planning to do, than to heal the afflicted, as he had done? Was it more righteous to have murder in the heart upon God's holy day, than to have love toward all men,— love, which finds expression in kindness and deeds of mercy?

In Jerusalem, by the sheep market, there was a pool called Bethesda. At certain times this pool was troubled; the people believed that an angel of the Lord went down into it, and stirred the waters, and that the first one who stepped in after the waters were stirred, would be cured of whatever disease he had.

Many visited the pool hoping to be healed; but only the first one who stepped in was benefited by it, and all the rest were disappointed.

One poor man had been afflicted by an incurable disease for thirty-eight years. He had many times visited the pool, but at each visit another would step in before him when the waters were troubled. His strength was about gone, and he felt that unless help came soon he must die.

"TAKE UP THY BED, AND WALK."

Jesus visited this place one day. He saw the sufferer gather his feeble energies in a last effort to reach the water. But, just as he had almost gained his object, another stepped in before him. In despair he crept back to his pallet to die. Hope had forsaken him, for he was sure he could not live until the water should be stirred again.

But a pitying face bent over him, saying : —

"Wilt thou be made whole?"

He answered, "Sir, I have no man, when the water is troubled, to put me into the pool; but while I am coming, another steppeth down before me."

Had the poor man only known it, there was One before him who could heal, not the first one only, but *all* who would come to him. With a voice of command Jesus said:—

"Rise, take up thy bed, and walk."

A sudden vigor animated the poor cripple. He bounded to his feet at the Saviour's command, and stooped to take up his bed, which was only a rug and a blanket. What a delight it was to stand upon his feet after so many weary years of helplessness.

As he hurried on toward Jerusalem, praising God and rejoicing in his new-found strength, he met the Pharisees, and told them the wonderful cure he had experienced. But instead of rejoicing with him, as he expected, they sternly reproved him for carrying his bed on the Sabbath day. The man feeling no guilt for this deed, boldly replied:—

"He that made me whole, the same said unto me, Take up thy bed, and walk." [9]

They excused the restored man from blame, but appeared shocked at the guilt of him who had assumed the responsibility of ordering a man to take up his bed upon the Sabbath day.

[9] John 5 : 1–11.

The Good Shepherd.

THE life of the Saviour was one of toil and deprivation. He was heard to say:—

"The foxes have holes, and the birds of the air have nests; but the Son of man hath not where to lay his head."[1]

But while he disregarded his own comfort, he was ever careful of others. As the watchful shepherd cares for his sheep, so he guarded his little flock of earthly followers. He said:—

"I am the good shepherd, and know my sheep, and am known of mine."

His love and care were not given to those only who were already in the fold, for he said, "The Son of man has come to save that which was lost."[2]

Again he said, "What man of you, having a hundred sheep, if he lose one of them, doth not leave the ninety and nine in the wilderness, and go after that which is lost, until he find it?

[1] Matthew 8:20,   [2] Matthew 18:11.

[59]

W. W. Robinson. Del.

"I Am the Good Shepherd."

"And when he hath found it, he layeth it on his shoulders, rejoicing. And when he cometh home, he calleth together his friends and neighbors, saying unto them, Rejoice with me ; for I have found my sheep which was lost.

"I say unto you, that likewise joy shall be in heaven over one sinner that repenteth, more than over ninety and nine just persons, which need no repentance."[3]

Let every wanderer from the fold take courage. The good Shepherd is searching for you. Remember that his work is "to save that which was lost." That means you. To doubt the possibility of your salvation is to doubt the saving power of Him who purchased you at an infinite cost. Let faith and hope take the place of doubt and unbelief. Look at the hands that were pierced for you, and believe in their power to save.

And when you accept the wonderful invitation, "there is joy in heaven." One more soul is rescued from the grasp of our great enemy,— the false shepherd. The Saviour announces to the heavenly host : —

"Rejoice with me ; for I have found my sheep which was lost."

And a joyful anthem rings out from the angelic choir, filling all heaven with richest melody.

Remember, halting, doubting one, God and Christ are interested in you, and all the hosts of heaven are engaged in the work of the salvation of sinners.

[3] Luke 15 : 4–7.

The wonderful miracles of the Saviour prove his power to save to the uttermost. The loathsome lepers were cleansed, the blind received their sight, the lame walked, and the deaf were made to hear.

The paralytic was made whole, and those afflicted with all manner of diseases were cured by a word from the Master. And even the devils were subject to him. They cried out : —

" Let us alone ; what have we to do with thee, thou Jesus of Nazareth ? art thou come to destroy us ? I know thee who thou art, the Holy One of God." [4]

But at the command of Jesus they were compelled to leave the poor souls whom they were possessing, and to come out of them. Those who witnessed these scenes were astonished, and said : —

" What a word is this ! for with authority and power he commandeth the unclean spirits, and they come out ? " [5]

Peter could walk the water at the command of his Lord until he took his eyes off from his Saviour, and then he began to doubt and sink. But when he cried, " Lord, save me ! " [6] the hand that never failed the one who called for help was stretched forth and rescued him from the wild billows.

Even the dead were raised to life. A clasp of the hand, and the words " Talitha cumi " [7] were sufficient to raise from the dead the daughter of Jairus.

[4] Mark 1 : 24.   [5] Luke 4 : 36.   [6] Matthew 14 : 30.   [7] Mark 5 . 41.

Lazarus was raised from the tomb by the voice of Jesus after he had been dead four days. And the funeral procession at Nain was stopped by Jesus, and the son of the widow was raised to life and health.

It was a wonderful work done by the Saviour during his ministry on earth. It was well defined in his answer sent to John the Baptist. John was in prison, and had become despondent, and even doubts troubled him as to whether Christ was indeed the Messiah. So he sent some of his followers to Jesus with the question : —

"Art thou he that should come, or do we look for another ?"

The messengers reached the Saviour while he was thronged with the sick and suffering, whom he was healing. At last he answered : —

"Go and shew John again those things which ye do hear and see : The blind received their sight, and the lame walk, the lepers are cleansed, and the deaf hear, the dead are raised up, and the poor have the gospel preached to them."[8]

For three years and a half the ministry of Jesus continued. Then, with his disciples, he went up to Jerusalem to be betrayed, condemned, and crucified.

[8] Matthew 11 : 3–5.

VIEWING JERUSALEM.

"Jesus halted, and a cloud of sorrow gathered upon his countenance."

Riding into Jerusalem.

JESUS was nearing Jerusalem to attend the passover. He was surrounded by multitudes who were also going up to this great yearly feast.

At his command, two of the disciples brought an ass's colt that he might ride into Jerusalem. They spread their garments upon the beast, and placed their Master upon it.

As soon as he was seated, a loud shout of triumph rent the air. The multitude hailed him as Messiah, their King. More than five hundred years before, the prophet had foretold this scene : —

"Rejoice greatly, O daughter of Zion ; . . . behold, thy King cometh unto thee ; . . . lowly, and riding upon an ass, and upon a colt the foal of an ass." [1]

All in the rapidly increasing throng were happy and excited. They could not offer him costly gifts, but they spread their outer garments, as a carpet, in his path. They broke off the beautiful branches of the olive and the palm, and strewed them in the way.

They thought they were escorting Jesus to take possession of the throne of David in Jerusalem.

The Saviour had never before allowed his followers to show him kingly honors. But at this time he desired especially to manifest himself to the world as its Redeemer.

The Son of God was about to become a sacrifice for the

sins of men. His church in all future ages must make his death a subject of deep thought and study. It was necessary, then, that the eyes of all people should now be directed to him.

After such a demonstration, his trial and crucifixion could never be hidden from the world. It was God's design that each event in the closing days of the Saviour's life should be so plainly marked that no power could cause it to be forgotten.

In the vast multitude surrounding the Saviour were the evidences of his miracle-working power.

The blind whom he had restored to sight were leading the way.

The dumb, whose tongues he had loosed, shouted the loudest hosannas.

The cripples whom he had healed leaped for joy, and were most active in breaking the palm branches and waving them before him.

Widows and orphans were exalting the name of Jesus for his works of mercy to them.

The loathsome lepers who had been cleansed by a word, spread their garments in the way.

Those who had been raised from the dead by the life-giving voice of the Saviour were there.

And Lazarus, whose body had seen corruption in the grave, but who was now enjoying the strength of glorious manhood, now joined the happy throng that was escorting the Saviour to Jerusalem.

As new numbers were added to the throng, they caught the inspiration of the hour, and joined in the shouts that echoed and re-echoed from hill to hill and from valley to valley : —

"Hosanna to the Son of David! Blessed is he that cometh in the name of the Lord! Hosanna in the highest!"[2]

Many Pharisees witnessed this scene, and were displeased. They felt that they were losing the con-

5 [2] Matthew 21:9.

trol of the people.   With all their authority they
tried to silence them; but their threats and appeals
only increased the enthusiasm.

Finding that they could not control the people,
they pressed through the crowd to where Jesus was,
and said to him: —

"Master, rebuke thy disciples."

They declared that such noisy demonstrations were
unlawful, and would not be permitted by the authorities.

Jesus answered, " I tell you that, if these should
hold their peace, the stones would immediately cry out."[3]

This triumphal entry was in God's order, and had
been foretold by the prophets, and no earthly power
could stop it.   The work of God will ever go forward, in spite of all that man may do to hinder or
tear it down.

As the procession came to the brow of the hill
overlooking Jerusalem, the full splendor of the city
met their view.   The vast multitude hushed their
shouts, spell-bound by the sudden vision of beauty.   All
eyes turn upon the Saviour, expecting to see in his
countenance the admiration which they themselves feel.

Jesus halted, and a cloud of sorrow gathered upon
his countenance, and the multitude were astonished to
see him burst into an agony of weeping.

Those who surrounded the Saviour could not understand his grief; but he wept for the city that was
doomed.   It had been the child of his care, and his

[3] Luke 19 : 39, 40.

heart was filled with anguish as he realized that it would soon be made desolate.

Had her people walked in the counsel of God, Jerusalem would have "stood forever." She might have be-

"THE CITY THAT WAS DOOMED."

come the queen of kingdoms, free in the strength of her God-given power. There would then have been no armed soldiers waiting at her gates, no Roman banners waving from her walls. From Jerusalem the dove of peace would have gone to all nations. She would have been the crowning glory of the world.

But they had rejected their Saviour, and were about to crucify their Redeemer. And when the sun should set that night, the doom of Jerusalem would be forever sealed.*

Reports had come to the rulers that Jesus was nearing the city with a vast company of followers.

---

*About forty years afterward, Jerusalem was utterly destroyed and burned with fire by the Roman army.

They went out to meet him, hoping to scatter the throng. With a show of much authority they asked : —

"Who is this?"[4]

The disciples, filled with a spirit of inspiration, answered : —

"Adam will tell you, It is the seed of the woman that shall bruise the serpent's head."

"Ask Abraham, he will tell you, It is Melchisedek, King of Salem, King of Peace."

"Jacob will tell you, He is Shiloh of the tribe of Judah."

"Isaiah will tell you, Immanuel, Wonderful, Counselor, the mighty God, the everlasting Father, the Prince of Peace."

"Jeremiah will tell you, The Branch of David, the Lord, our righteousness."

"Daniel will tell you, He is the Messiah."

"Hosea will tell you, He is the Lord God of Hosts, the Lord is his memorial."

"John the Baptist will tell you, He is the Lamb of God who taketh away the sin of the world."

"The great Jehovah has proclaimed from his throne, This is my beloved Son."

"We his disciples, declare, This is Jesus, the Messiah, the Prince of Life, the Redeemer."

"And even the prince of the power of darkness acknowledges him, saying, I know thee who thou art, the Holy One of God!"

[4] Matthew 21 : 10.

"Take These Things Hence."

THE next day Jesus entered the temple. Here he found the same scene of buying and selling that he had rebuked so sharply three years before. As on the previous occasion, the court of the temple was filled with cattle, sheep, and birds. These were kept for sale to those who desired to buy them for offerings for their sins.

Extortion and robbery were practiced by those engaged in this unholy traffic. So great was the babel of sounds from the court that it seriously disturbed the worshipers within.

Again the piercing look of the Saviour swept over the court of the temple. All eyes were turned toward him. The voices of the people and the noise of the cattle were hushed. All looked with astonishment and awe upon the Son of God. The divine flashed through the human, and gave Jesus a dignity and glory he had never exhibited before. The silence became almost unbearable. Finally the Saviour spoke

CLEANSING THE TEMPLE.

"Take these things hence."

in clear tones, and with a power that swayed the people like a mighty tempest : —

"It is written, My house is the house of prayer ; but ye have made it a den of thieves."[1]

With still greater authority than he had manifested three years before, he commanded : —

"Take these things hence."

Once before the priests and rulers of the temple had fled at the sound of this voice. Afterward they were ashamed of having done so. They felt that they would never surrender in this manner again. Yet a second time they were more terrified, and in greater haste than before to obey his command, and they fled from the temple, driving their cattle before them.

The court of the temple was almost immediately filled with those bringing their sick and suffering to be healed by Jesus. Some were in a dying condition. These afflicted ones felt their distressing need. They fixed their eyes imploringly upon the face of Christ, fearing there to see the severity which had driven out the buyers and sellers. But they saw in his face only love and tender pity.

Jesus kindly received the sick, and disease and suffering fled at the touch of his hand. He tenderly gathered the children in his arms, soothed their fretful cries, banished sickness and pain from their little forms, and handed them back, smiling and healthful, to their mothers.

[1] Luke 19 : 46.

What a scene to greet the priests and rulers as they cautiously made their way back to the temple! They heard the voices of men, women, and children praising God. They saw the sick healed, the blind restored to sight, the deaf receive their hearing, and the lame leap for joy.

The children took the lead in these rejoicings. They repeated the

"Out of the mouths of babes and sucklings thou hast perfected praise"

hosannas of the day before, and waved palm branches before the Saviour. The temple echoed and re-echoed with their shouts : —

"Hosanna to the Son of David!"

"Blessed is He that cometh in the name of the Lord!"[2]

"Behold, thy King cometh unto thee; he is just, and having salvation."[3]

[2] Matthew 21 : 9.   [3] Zechariah 9 : 9.

The rulers tried to silence the shouts of the happy children, but all were filled with joy and praise for the wonderful works of Jesus, and would not be stopped.

The rulers then turned to the Saviour, hoping that he would command them to cease. They said to him : —

"Hearest thou what these say?"

Jesus replied, "Yea; have ye never read, Out of the mouth of babes and sucklings thou hast perfected praise?"[4]

The blessed privilege of heralding the birth of Christ and forwarding his work in the earth had been refused by the haughty rulers of the people. His praises must be sounded ; and God chose the children to do it. Had the voices of those rejoicing children been silenced, the very pillars of the temple would have cried out in the Saviour's praise.

[4] Matthew 21 : 16.

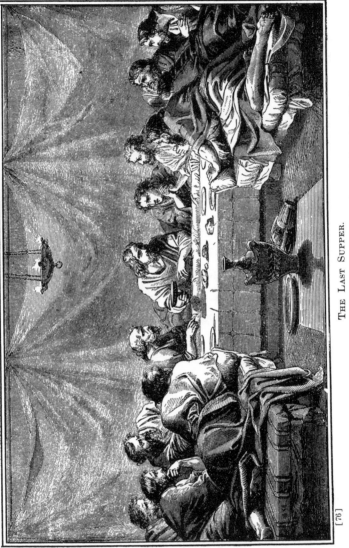

THE LAST SUPPER.

"With desire I have desired to eat this passover with you before I suffer."

The Passover Supper.

HE day on which the passover was to be kept had now come. And Jesus bade Peter and John find a place, and prepare the passover supper.

He told these disciples that when they were gone into the street, they should meet a man bearing a pitcher of water.

Him they were to follow, and enter into the house where he entered. And they were to say to the goodman of that house : —

"The Master saith unto thee, Where is the guest chamber, where I shall eat the passover with my disciples ?"[1]

This man would then show them a large upper room furnished for their needs. There they were to make ready the passover supper. And it all happened just as the Saviour had told them that it would.

The passover suppers which the disciples had eaten with their Master had always been seasons of deep

[1] Luke 22 : 11.

interest to them. But upon this occasion Jesus was troubled in spirit.

His heart was wrung with grief as he thought of the cruelty and ingratitude which those he came to save would show to him.

At length he said to the disciples in tones of touching sadness : —

" With desire I have desired to eat this passover with you before I suffer." [2]

This was in reality the last passover that was ever to be kept. The Lamb of God was now to be slain for the sins of the world, and when the Jews sealed their rejection of Christ by putting him to death, they rejected all that gave this feast its true value and significance.

And Jesus " took the cup, and gave thanks, and said : —

" Take this, and divide it among yourselves ; for I say unto you, I will not drink of the fruit of the vine, until the kingdom of God shall come."

At this passover supper, Jesus gave his disciples a lesson in humility. A dispute had previously risen among them as to which of them should be greatest in Christ's kingdom.

Having girded himself like a servant, the Saviour washed the feet of his disciples. When he had finished, he said to them : —

[2] Luke 22 : 15.

"If I then, your Lord and Master, have washed your feet; ye also ought to wash one another's feet. For I have given you an example, that ye should do as I have done to you."[3]

The disciples were thus taught that, instead of quarreling for a high place, each should count the other better than himself.

"And he took bread, and gave thanks, and brake it, and gave unto them, saying: —

"This is my body, which is given for you; this do in remembrance of me."

And after supper he took the cup, saying: —

"This cup is the new testament [covenant] in my blood, which is shed for you."[4]

As the disciples sat at the table with their Master, they noticed that he seemed greatly troubled. A cloud settled over them all, and they ate in silence.

Finally Jesus spoke, and said: —

"Verily I say unto you, that one of you shall betray me."

The disciples were grieved and amazed at these words. Each began to look into his heart to see if there were any shadow of an evil thought against the Master.

One after another they asked, "Lord, is it I?"[5]

Judas alone remained silent. This drew the eyes

[3] John 13 : 14. [4] Luke 22 : 17-20. [5] Matthew 26 : 21, 22.

of all to him. When he saw that he was observed, he too asked, "Lord, is it I?"

And Jesus solemnly replied, "Thou hast said."[6]

When Judas thus saw that his evil purpose was known, he arose hastily to leave the room. As he went out, Jesus said:—

"That thou doest, do quickly."[7]

The going of Judas was a relief to all present. The Saviour's face lighted, and at this the shadow was lifted from the disciples.

Jesus had many things to say to his disciples before he left them. With the deepest interest he poured forth the burden of his soul in words of comfort, counsel, and prayer. These words were a support to the disciples in their time of trial.

[6] Matthew 26: 25   [7] John 13: 27.

In Gethsemane.

THE Saviour, during his ministry, often spent whole nights in earnest prayer to his Father. It was by so doing that he obtained strength and wisdom to sustain him in his work, and keep him from falling under the temptations of Satan.

After eating the passover supper with his disciples, Jesus went with them to the garden of Gethsemane, where he often went to pray. As they walked, the Master conversed with them, and instructed them ; but as they neared the garden, he became strangely silent.

All his life, Christ had lived in the presence of his Father. The Spirit of God had been his constant guide and support. He always gave God the glory for his works on earth, and said, "I can of mine own self do nothing."[1]

We can do nothing of ourselves. It is only by relying on Jesus for all our strength that we can overcome, and do his will on earth. We must have the same simple, childlike trust in him that he had in his

COS-6   [1] John 5 : 30.

THE AGONY IN THE GARDEN

"O my Father, if this cup may not pass away from me, except I drink it,
thy will be done."

Father. Jesus said, "For without me ye can do nothing." [2]

The terrible night of agony for the Saviour began as they neared the garden. It seemed that the presence of God which had been his support was no longer with him. He was beginning to feel what it was to be shut out from his Father.

Christ must bear the sins of the world. As they were now laid upon him, they seemed more than he could endure. The guilt of sin was so terrible, he was tempted to fear that God would no longer love him.

As the awful displeasure of the Father against evil was felt, the words were forced from him, "My soul is exceeding sorrowful, even unto death." In his sorrow and suffering he turned to his disciples for comfort and support.

Near the gate of the garden, Jesus had left all his disciples except Peter, James, and John, and had gone into the garden with these three. They were his most earnest followers, and the most to be relied upon. But he could not bear that even they should witness the suffering that was to be pressed upon him. He said to them : —

"Tarry ye here, and watch with me." [3]

He went a short distance from them, and fell prostrate upon the ground. He felt that he was being separated by sin from the Father. The gulf between

[2] John 15 : 5.

6

[3] Matthew 26 : 38.

them appeared so broad, so black, so deep, that he feared for the result.

Christ was not suffering for his own sins, but for the sins of the world. He was feeling the displeasure of God against sin as the sinner will feel it in the great reckoning day.

In his agony, Christ clung to the cold ground. From his pale lips came the bitter cry, " O my Father, if it be possible, let this cup pass from me ; nevertheless not as I will, but as thou wilt." [4]

For an hour Jesus bore this terrible suffering alone. Then he came to the disciples for sympathy ; but no sympathy awaited him, for they were fast asleep. They awoke at the voice of Jesus, but hardly knew him, his face was so changed by anguish.

Jesus said to Peter, " Simon, sleepest thou ? couldest thou not watch one hour ? " [5] A little while before, Peter had declared that he could go with his Lord to

[4] Matthew 26 : 39.   [5] Mark 14 : 37.

prison and to death. Yet in this hour of agony and temptation, he fell quietly asleep.

John, the loving disciple, who had leaned on the breast of Jesus, was also wrapped in slumber. Surely the love of John for his Master, should have kept him awake! The Redeemer had prayed whole nights for his disciples, that their faith might not fail them in the hour of trial. Yet they could not remain awake with him a single hour.

Had Jesus now asked James and John, "Can ye drink of the cup that I drink of? and be baptized with the baptism that I am baptized with?" they would not have answered so readily as they did before, "We can."[6]

The heart of Jesus was filled with pity and sympathy at the weakness of his disciples. He feared that they could not endure the test that his suffering and death would bring upon them.

Yet he did not sternly reprove them for their weakness. He thought of the trials before them, and said to them : —

"Watch and pray, that ye enter not into temptation."

He made an excuse for their failure in duty toward him : "The spirit indeed is willing, but the flesh is weak."[7] What an example of the tender, loving pity of the Saviour!

[6] Mark 10 : 38, 39. [7] Matthew 26 : 41.

Again the Son of God was seized with superhuman agony. Fainting and exhausted, he staggered back, and prayed as before : —

"O my Father, if this cup may not pass away from me, except I drink it, thy will be done." [8]

The agony of this prayer forced drops of blood from his pores. Again he sought the disciples for sympathy, and again he found them sleeping. His presence aroused them. They looked upon his face with fear, for it was stained with blood. They could not understand the anguish of mind which his face expressed.

The third time he sought the place of prayer. A horror of great darkness overcame him. He had lost the presence of his Father. Without this, he feared that in his human nature he could not endure the test.

The third time he prays the same prayer as before. Angels are anxious to bring relief, but it may not be. The Son of God must drink this cup, or the world will be lost forever. He sees the helplessness of man. He sees the power of sin. The woes of a doomed world pass in review before him.

He makes the final decision. He will save man at any cost to himself. Again he prays : —

"If this cup may not pass away from me, except I drink it, thy will be done."

The prayer of the Saviour now breathes only submission. He falls dying to the ground, but a shin-

[8] Matthew 26 : 42.

ing angel is now permitted to minister to him. He lifts the head of the divine sufferer, and points toward heaven. He tells him that he has come off victor over Satan. As the result, millions will be victors in his glorious kingdom.

A heavenly peace now rested upon the Saviour's blood-stained face. He sought his disciples, and again found them sleeping. Had they remained awake, watching and praying with their Saviour, they would have received help for the trial before them. Missing this, they had no strength in their hour of need.

Looking sorrowfully on them, Jesus said, "Sleep on now, and take your rest; behold, the hour is at hand, and the Son of man is betrayed into the hands of sinners."

Even as he spoke these words, he heard the foot-steps of the mob in search of him, and said : —

"Rise, let us be going; behold, he is at hand that doth betray me."[9]

[9] Matthew 26 : 45, 46.

The Betrayal and Arrest.

NO traces of his recent suffering were to be seen as the Saviour stepped forth to meet his betrayer. Standing in advance of his disciples, he asked the mob : —

"Whom seek ye?"

They answered, "Jesus of Nazareth."

Jesus replied, "I am He."[1]

As Jesus spoke these words, the angel who had recently ministered to him moved between him and the mob. A divine light illuminated the Saviour's face, and a dove-like form overshadowed him.

The murderous throng could not stand a moment in the presence of this divine glory. They staggered back. The priests, elders, and soldiers dropped as dead men to the ground.

The angel withdrew, and the light faded away. Jesus could have escaped, but he remained, calm and self-possessed. His disciples were too much amazed to utter a word.

[1] John 18 : 5.

The Roman soldiers soon started to their feet. With the priests and Judas, they gathered about Christ. They seemed ashamed of their weakness, and fearful that he would escape. Again the question was asked by the Redeemer:—

The Traitor's Kiss

"Whom seek ye?"

Again they answered, "Jesus of Nazareth."

The Saviour then said, "I have told you that I am he. If therefore ye seek me, let these [pointing to his disciples] go their way."[2]

In this hour of trial, Christ's thoughts were for his beloved disciples. He did not wish to have them suffer, even though he must go to prison and to death.

Judas, the false disciple, did not forget the part he was to act. He came close to Jesus, and bestowed upon him the traitor's kiss.

[2] John 18: 7, 8

Jesus said to him, "Friend, wherefore art thou come?"[3] His voice trembled as he added, "Betrayest thou the Son of man with a kiss?"[4]

These gentle words should have touched the heart of Judas; but all tenderness and honor seemed to have left him. Judas had allowed Satan to take possession of him. He stood boldly before the Lord, and showed no desire to save him from the cruel mob.

Jesus did not refuse the traitor's kiss. In this he gave us an example of forbearance, love, and pity. If we are his disciples, we must treat our enemies as Jesus did Judas.

The murderous throng became bold as they saw Judas touch the form which had so recently been glorified before their eyes. They now laid hold of Jesus, and bound those hands that had ever been employed in doing good.

The disciples did not think Jesus would allow himself to be taken. They knew that the power that could strike down the mob as dead men, could preserve their Master from his enemies.

They were disappointed and indignant as they saw the cords brought forward to bind the hands of Him whom they loved. Peter, in his anger, drew his sword and rashly cut off an ear of the servant of the high priest.

When Jesus saw what Peter had done, he released his hands, though held firmly by the Roman soldiers,

[3] Matthew 26: 50.   [4] Luke 22: 48.

and saying, "Suffer ye thus far,"[5] he touched the wounded ear, and it was instantly made whole.

He then said to Peter, "Put up again thy sword into his place; for all they that take the sword shall perish with the sword. Thinkest thou that I cannot now pray to my Father, and he shall presently give me more than twelve legions of angels? But how then shall the scriptures be fulfilled, that thus it must be?"[6] "The cup which my Father hath given me, shall I not drink it?"[7]

Jesus then turned to the chief priest and the captains of the temple, who helped compose that murderous throng, and said, "Are ye come out, as against a thief, with swords and with staves to take me? I was daily with you in the temple teaching, and ye took me not; but the scripture must be fulfilled."[8]

The disciples were offended when they saw that Jesus made no effort to deliver himself from his enemies. They blamed him for not doing so. They could not understand his submission to the mob, and, terror-stricken, they forsook him and fled.

In the upper chamber Christ had foretold this scene. "Behold, the hour cometh, yea, is now come, that ye shall be scattered, every man to his own, and shall leave me alone; and yet I am not alone, because the Father is with me."[9]

[5] Luke 22 : 51.   [6] Matthew 26 : 52–54.   [7] John 18 : 11.
[8] Mark 14 : 48, 49.   [9] John 16 : 32.

BEFORE THE SANHEDRIM.

"He is brought as a lamb to the slaughter, and as a sheep before her shearers is dumb, so he openeth not his mouth."

Before Annas, Caiaphas, and the Sanhedrim.

JESUS was followed from the garden of Gethsemane by the hooting mob. He moved painfully, for his hands were tightly bound and he was closely guarded.

He was taken first to the house of Annas, the father-in-law of Caiaphas, who was the high priest that year. The wicked Annas had requested that he might be the first to see Jesus of Nazareth a bound captive. From this place he was hurried to the palace of Caiaphas.

While the members of the Sanhedrim, the chief council of the Jews, were being called together, Annas and Caiaphas questioned Jesus, hoping to gain evidence by which to secure his condemnation.

The high priest first questioned him in regard to his disciples and his doctrine. To this Jesus answered : —

"I spake openly to the world; I ever taught in the synagogue, and in the temple, whither the Jews always resort; and in secret have I said nothing."

Then, turning upon the questioner, Jesus said, " Why askest thou me ? Ask them which heard me, what I have said." [1]

These very priests had set spies to watch him and report his every word. Through these spies the priests and rulers knew of his sayings and of his works at every gathering of the people he had attended. These spies had sought to entrap the Master in his word that they might find something by which to condemn him. So the Saviour said, " Ask them which heard me." Go to your spies. They heard all that I have said. They can tell you what my teaching has been.

The words of Jesus were so searching and pointed that the high priest felt that his prisoner was reading his very soul.

But one of the servants of the high priest, assuming that his master was not being treated with proper respect, struck Jesus in the face, saying : —

" Answerest thou the high priest so ? "

To this insulting question and blow, Jesus mildly said : —

" If I have spoken evil, bear witness of the evil ; but if well, why smitest thou me ? " [2]

Jesus could have summoned legions of angels from heaven to his aid. But it was a part of his mission to endure in his humanity all the taunts and insults that humanity might heap upon him.

[1] John 18: 20, 21.   [2] John 18: 22, 23.

When the members of the Sanhedrim assembled, Caiaphas took his seat as presiding officer. On either side were the judges, and the Roman soldiers stood before them, guarding the Saviour. Back of them was the accusing mob.

Caiaphas then asked Jesus to work one of his mighty miracles before them. But the Saviour gave no sign that he heard the request. Had he responded by even one soul-searching look, such as he gave the buyers and sellers in the temple, the whole murderous throng would have been compelled to fly from his presence.

The Jews at this time were subject to the Romans, and were not allowed to punish any one with death. The Sanhedrim could not even pass the death sentence. They could only condemn the prisoner, and collect such evidence to present to the Roman governor, as would lead him to pass the sentence of death.

To accomplish their wicked purpose, they must find something against the Saviour that would be regarded as criminal by the Roman power. They could secure abundant evidence that Christ had spoken against the Jewish traditions and many of their ordinances. It was easy to prove that he had denounced the priests and scribes, and that he had called them hypocrites and murderers. But this would not be listened to by the Romans, for they were themselves disgusted with the pretensions of the Pharisees.

Many charges were brought against Jesus, but either the witnesses disagreed, or the evidence was of such a nature that it would not be accepted by the Romans. They tried to make him speak in answer to their accusations, but he appeared as if he had not heard them.   The silence of Christ at this time had been thus described by the prophet Isaiah : —

"He was oppressed, and he was afflicted, yet he opened not his mouth, he is brought as a lamb to the slaughter, and as a sheep before her shearers is dumb, so he openeth not his mouth."[3]

The priests began to fear they would fail of obtaining any evidence which they could use against their prisoner when they should take him to Pilate. They felt that one last effort must be made.   The high priest raised his right hand toward heaven, and addressed Jesus in the form of a solemn oath : —

"I adjure thee by the living God, that thou tell us whether thou be the Christ, the Son of God."[4]

[3] Isaiah 53 : 7.   [4] Matthew 26 : 63.

Jesus never denied his mission or his relation to the Father.   He could remain silent to personal insult, but he ever spoke plainly and decidedly when his work or his Sonship to God were brought in question.

Every ear was bent to listen, and every eye was fixed upon him as he answered : —

" Thou hast said."

In the custom of those days this was the same as answering.   " Yes," or, " It is as thou hast said." This was the strongest form of an affirmative answer. A heavenly light seemed to illuminate the pale countenance of the Saviour as he added : —

" Nevertheless I say unto you, Hereafter shall ye see the Son of Man sitting on the right hand of power, and coming in the clouds of heaven." [5]

In this statement the Saviour presented the reverse of the scene then taking place.   He pointed forward to the time when he shall occupy the position of supreme judge of heaven and earth.   He will then be seated upon the Father's throne, and from his decisions there will be no appeal.

He brought before them a view of that day, when instead of being surrounded and abused by a riotous mob, he will come in the clouds of heaven with power and great glory.   Then he will be escorted by legions of angels.   Then he will pronounce sentence upon his enemies, among whom will be that same accusing throng.

[5] Matthew 26 : 64.

As Jesus spake the words declaring himself to be the Son of God, the judge of the world, the high priest rent his clothes to show his horror at the blasphemy uttered by Christ.   He lifted his hands toward heaven, and said : —

"He hath spoken blasphemy ; what further need

"HE IS GUILTY, PUT HIM
TO DEATH !"

have we of witnesses ? behold, now ye have heard his blasphemy.   What think ye ?"   The judges answered, "He is guilty of death."[6]

When the condemnation of Jesus was thus pronounced by the judges, a satanic fury took possession of the people.   The roar of voices was like that of wild beasts.

They made a rush toward Jesus, crying, He is guilty, put him to death ! and had it not been for the

[6] Matthew 26 : 65, 66.

soldiers, he would have been torn into pieces before his judges. But Roman authority interfered, and by force of arms withheld the violence of the mob.

The priests and rulers, together with wicked men, now joined in abusing the Saviour. An old garment was thrown over his head; and his persecutors struck him in the face, saying: —

"Prophesy unto us, thou Christ, Who is he that smote thee?" [7]

When the garment was removed, one poor wretch spat in the Saviour's face.

The angels of God faithfully recorded every insulting look, word, and act against their beloved Commander. One day those base men who scorned and spat upon the calm, pale face of Christ, will look upon it in its glory, shining brighter than the sun.

[7] Matthew 26 : 68.

JUDAS SELLING CHRIST.

"He could now sell his Lord for thirty pieces of silver."

Judas.

THE Jewish rulers were anxious to get Jesus into their power, but they did not dare to take him openly, for fear of raising a tumult among the people. So they sought some one who would secretly betray him, and found the man who would do this base act in Judas, one of the twelve disciples.

Judas had naturally a strong love for money, but he had not always been wicked and corrupt enough to do such a deed as this. He had fostered the evil spirit of avarice until it had become the ruling motive of his life, and he could now sell his Lord for thirty pieces of silver, which was about seventeen dollars. He could now betray the Saviour with a kiss at Gethsemane.

But he followed every step of the Son of God as he went from the garden to the trial before the Jewish rulers. He had no thought that the Saviour would allow the Jews to kill him, as they had threatened to do.

At every movement he expected to see him released, and protected by divine power, as had been done in the past. But as the hours went by, and Jesus quietly submitted to all the indignities that were heaped upon him, a terrible fear came to the traitor, that he had indeed betrayed his Master to his death.

As the trial drew to a close, Judas could endure the torture of his guilty conscience no longer. All at once a hoarse voice rang through the hall, which sent a thrill of terror to the hearts of all present : —

"He is innocent. Spare him, O Caiaphas. He has done nothing worthy of death!"

The tall form of Judas was now seen pressing through the startled crowd. His face was pale and haggard, and large drops of sweat stood upon his forehead. He rushed to the throne of judgment, and threw down before the high priest the pieces of silver he had received as the price of his Lord's betrayal.

He eagerly grasped the robe of Caiaphas, and implored him to release Jesus, declaring that he was innocent of all crime. Caiaphas angrily shook him off, and answered with chilling scorn : —

"What is that to us? see thou to that."[1]

Finding his prayers were in vain, Judas fell at the feet of Jesus, acknowledging him to be the Son of God, begging forgiveness for his sin, and imploring him to exercise his godlike power, and deliver himself from his enemies.

[1] Matthew 27 : 4.

The Saviour did not reproach his betrayer either by look or word. He knew that he was suffering the bitterest remorse for his sin. He gazed compassionately upon Judas, and said : —

" For this hour came I into the world."

A murmur of surprise ran through the assembly at the heavenly forbearance of the Saviour.

Perceiving that his entreaties did not release the prisoner, Judas rushed from the hall, crying : —

" It is too late ! It is too late ! "

He felt that he could not live to see Jesus crucified, and, in an agony of remorse, went out and hanged himself.

Later that same day, on the road from Pilate's judgment hall to Calvary, there came an interruption to the shouts and jeers of the wicked throng who were leading Jesus to the place of crucifixion. As they passed a retired spot, they saw at the foot of a lifeless tree the dead body of Judas.

It was a most revolting scene. His weight had broken the cord by which he had hanged himself to the tree. In falling, his body had been horribly mangled, and dogs were now devouring it.

His remains were immediately buried out of sight ; but there was less mockery, and many a pale face revealed the fearful thoughts within. Retribution seemed already to be visiting those who were guilty of the blood of Jesus.

Before Pilate.

AFTER Jesus had been condemned by the judges of the Sanhedrim, he was taken at once to Pilate, the Roman governor, to have the sentence confirmed and executed.

The Jewish priests and rulers could not themselves enter the judgment hall of Pilate. By the ceremonial laws of their nation, they would become defiled by so doing, and thus be debarred from taking part in the feast of the passover.

In their blindness they could not see that Christ was the real passover Lamb, and that when they put him to death, this great feast would lose all its meaning.

As Pilate beheld Jesus, he saw a man of noble countenance and dignified bearing. No trace of crime was to be seen in his face. Pilate turned to the priests and asked : —

"What accusation bring ye against this man?"[1]

His accusers did not want to state particulars, and so were not prepared for this question. They knew that they could not bring any truthful evidence on which the Roman governor would condemn him. So

"Art Thou the King of the Jews?"

the priests called the false witnesses to their aid. "And they began to accuse him, saying: —

"We found this fellow perverting the nation, and forbidding to give tribute to Cæsar, saying that he himself is Christ a King."[2]

This was false, for Jesus himself had paid tribute, and had taught his disciples to do so. When the

[1] John 18: 29. [2] Luke 23: 2.

lawyers had tried to entrap him in regard to this very matter, he had said : —

" Render therefore unto Cæsar the things which are Cæsar's." [3]

Pilate was not deceived by this false testimony. He turned to the Saviour, and asked : —

" Art thou the king of the Jews ? "

Jesus answered, " Thou sayest." [4]

When they heard this answer, Caiaphas and those who were with him called Pilate to witness that Jesus had admitted the crime of which they accused him. With noisy cries, they demanded that he be sentenced to death.

As Christ made no answer to his accusers, Pilate said to him : —

" Answerest thou nothing ? behold how many things they witness against thee ?

" But Jesus yet answered nothing." [5]

Pilate was perplexed. He saw no evidence of crime in Jesus, and he had no confidence in those who were accusing him. The noble appearance and the quiet manner of the Son of God were in direct contrast to the excitement and fury of his accusers. Pilate was impressed with this, and was well satisfied of the innocence of Jesus.

Hoping to gain the truth from the Saviour, he took him into his house, and questioned him : —

[3] Matthew 22 : 21.   [4] Matthew 27 : 11.   [5] Mark 15 : 4, 5.

"Art thou the King of the Jews?"

Christ did not give a direct answer to Pilate, but asked:—

"Sayest thou this thing of thyself, or did others tell it thee of me?"

The Spirit of God was striving with Pilate. The question of Jesus was intended to lead him to examine his own heart more closely. Pilate understood the meaning of the question. His own heart was opened before him, and he saw that his soul was stirred by conviction. But pride arose in his heart, and he answered:—

"Am I a Jew? Thine own nation and the chief priests have delivered thee unto me; what hast thou done?"

Pilate's golden opportunity had passed. Jesus desired Pilate to understand that he did not come to be an earthly king, and so said to him:—

"My kingdom is not of this world; if my kingdom were of this world, then would my servants fight, that I should not be delivered to the Jews; but now is my kingdom not from hence."

Pilate then asked him, "Art thou a king then?

"Jesus answered, Thou sayest that I am a king. To this end was I born, and for this cause came I into the world, that I should bear witness unto the truth. Every one that is of the truth heareth my voice."

Pilate had a desire to know the truth. Ideas of truth in the religious world were divided then, as they are now. His mind was confused. He eagerly grasped the words of the Saviour, and his heart was stirred with a great longing to know what it really was, and how he could obtain it. He asked Jesus : —

"What is truth ? "

But Pilate did not wait for an answer. The tumult of the crowd outside the hall of justice had increased to a roar. He was recalled from his position as learner at the feet of Christ, to that of the Roman Governor. He went out to the people, and declared in a positive voice : —

"I find in him no fault at all."[6]

These words from a heathen judge were a scathing rebuke to the base perfidy and falsehood of the rulers of Israel who were accusing the Saviour.

As the priests and elders heard this from Pilate, their disappointment and rage knew no bounds. They had long plotted and waited for this opportunity. As they saw the prospect of the release of Jesus, they seemed ready to tear him in pieces.

They lost all reason and self-control, and gave vent to curses, behaving more like demons than men. They loudly denounced Pilate, and threatened him with the censure of the Roman Government. They accused Pilate of refusing to condemn Jesus, who, they affirmed,

[6] John 18 : 33–38.

had set himself up against Cæsar. They then set up the cry : —

" He stirreth up the people, teaching throughout all Jewry, beginning from Galilee to this place." [7]

Pilate at this time had no thought of condemning Jesus. He was sure of his innocence. But when he heard that Christ was from Galilee, he decided to send him to Herod, who was ruler of that province, and was in Jerusalem at that time. By this course, Pilate thought to shift the responsibility of the trial from himself to Herod.

Jesus was faint from hunger, and weary from loss of sleep. He was also suffering from the cruel treatment he had received. But Pilate delivered him again to the soldiers, and he was dragged away, amid the jeers and insults of the merciless mob.

[7] Luke 23 : 5.

MOCKING THE SAVIOUR.

"He submitted to the coarsest insult and outrage with dignified composure."

Copyright 1895 by Johnson Smith & Trade Co.

Before Herod.

WITHOUT delay Jesus was hurried to the judgment hall of Herod. Herod had never met Jesus, but he had long desired to see him, and witness his marvelous power. As the Saviour was brought before him, the rabble surged and pressed about, some crying one thing and some another. Herod commanded silence, for he wished to question the prisoner.

He looked with curiosity and pity upon the pale face of Christ. He saw there the marks of deep wisdom and purity. He was satisfied, as Pilate had been, that malice and envy alone had caused the Jews to accuse the Saviour.

Herod urged Jesus to perform one of his wonderful miracles before him. He promised to release him if he would do so. By his direction crippled and deformed persons were brought in, and, in a voice of authority, he commanded Jesus to heal them. But the Saviour stood before Herod as one who neither saw nor heard.

The Son of God had taken upon himself the nature of man. He must do as man must do in similar circumstances. Therefore he would not work a miracle to gratify curiosity, or to save himself the pain and humiliation that man must endure when placed as he was.

His accusers were terrified when Herod demanded of Christ a miracle. Of all things, they dreaded most an exhibition of his divine power. Such a manifestation would be a death blow to their plans, and would perhaps cost them their lives. So they set up the cry that Jesus worked miracles through the power given him by Beelzebub, the prince of devils.

Earlier in his life, Herod had very nearly become a disciple of John; but he failed to heed the warnings of the prophet, and continued in his life of intemperance and sin. Finally he came where he could command that John should be slain, and his head brought to the wicked Herodias.

Now his heart had become still more hardened. He could not bear the silence of Jesus. His face grew dark with passion, and he angrily threatened the Saviour, who still remained unmoved and silent.

Jesus had ever been ready to listen to the earnest plea of even the worst sinners; but he had no ear for the command of Herod. His heart, ever touched by the presence of human woe, was closed to the haughty king who felt no need of a Saviour.

In anger, Herod turned to the multitude, and denounced Jesus as an impostor. But the accusers of the Saviour knew that he was no impostor. They had seen too many of his mighty works to believe this charge.

Then the king began to shamefully abuse and ridicule the Son of God. "And Herod with his men of war set him at naught, and mocked him, and arrayed him in a gorgeous robe."

As the wicked king saw Jesus accepting all this indignity in silence, he was moved with a sudden fear that this was no common man before him. He was perplexed with the thought that his prisoner might be a god come down to earth.

Herod did not dare to ratify the condemnation of the Jews. He wished to relieve himself of the terrible responsibility, and so sent Jesus back to Pilate.

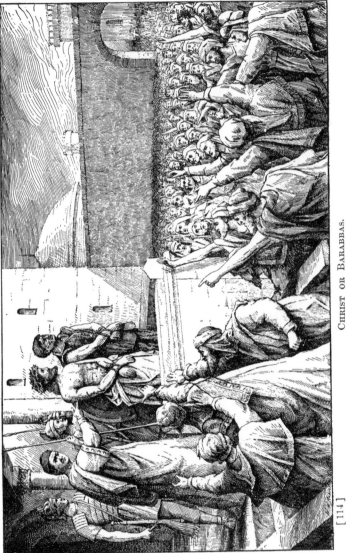

CHRIST OR BARABBAS.

"Away with this man, and release unto us Barabbas."

Condemned by Pilate.

WHEN the Jews returned from Herod, bringing the Saviour again to Pilate, he was very much displeased, and asked what they would have him do. He reminded them that he had examined Jesus, and had found no fault in him. He told them that they had brought complaints against him, but that they had not been able to prove a single charge.

And, furthermore, they had taken him to Herod, who was a Jew, like themselves, and he had found in him nothing worthy of death. But to pacify the accusers, he said : —

"I will therefore chastise him, and release him."[1]

Here Pilate showed his weakness. He had acknowledged that Christ was innocent; then why should he punish him? It was a compromise with wrong. The Jews never forgot this through all the trial. They had intimidated the Roman governor, and now pressed their advantage until they secured the condemnation of Jesus.

The multitude clamored more loudly for the life of the prisoner. Jesus could no longer endure the

[1] Luke 23 : 16.

strain put upon him, and fell exhausted to the marble pavement. It was at this moment that a messenger brought a letter to Pilate from his wife, which read : —

"Have thou nothing to do with that just man : for I have suffered many things this day in a dream because of him."[2]

Pilate turned pale at this message ; but the mob became more urgent as they saw his indecision. They were wrought up to a state of insane fury.

The governor was compelled to act. It was customary at the feast of the passover to set at liberty some one prisoner that the people might select. The Roman soldiers had recently captured a noted robber, named Barabbas. He was a degraded ruffian and a murderer. So Pilate turned to the crowd, and said with great earnestness : —

"Whom will ye that I release unto you ? Barabbas, or Jesus which is called Christ ?"[3]

They replied, "Away with this man, and release unto us Barabbas."[4]

Pilate was dumb with surprise and disappointment. By yielding his own judgment, and appealing to the people, he had lost his dignity and the control of the crowd. He was, after that, only the tool of the mob. They swayed him at their will. He then asked : —

"What shall I do then with Jesus which is called Christ ?"

[2] Matthew 27 : 19.   [3] Matthew 27 : 17.   [4] Luke 23 : 18.

With one accord they cried, " Let him be crucified.

" And the governor said, Why, what evil hath he done ?

" But they cried out the more, saying, Let him be crucified."[5]

Pilate's cheek paled as he heard the terrible cry, " Crucify him ! " He had not thought it would come to that. He had repeatedly pronounced Jesus innocent, and yet the people were determined that he should suffer this most terrible and dreaded death. Again he asked the question : —

" Why, what evil hath he done ? "

And again the awful cry was set up, " Crucify him ! "

Pilate made one last effort to touch their sympathies. Jesus was taken, faint with weariness and covered with wounds, and scourged in the sight of his accusers.

Stripped to the waist, his back showed the long, cruel stripes, from which the blood was still flowing. His gentle face showed the marks of the terrible ordeal through which he had passed.

The low-browed, vicious Barabbas was then brought and placed by the side of the Son of God, that all might see the contrast in the men between whom they had made their choice. Pointing to the two, Pilate said, in a voice of solemn entreaty : —

[5] Matthew 27 : 22, 23.

"Behold the man."

There were men of intelligence before Pilate. They could read as well as he, the look of nobility and purity in the pale, suffering face of the Saviour. But they were lost to all reason, and to every feeling of justice or compassion, and replied: —

"Crucify him, crucify him!"

At last, losing all patience with their

"I AM INNOCENT OF THE BLOOD OF THIS JUST PERSON."

unreasonable, vengeful cruelty, Pilate said to them: —

"Take ye him, and crucify him; for I find no fault in him."[6]

Pilate tried hard to release the Saviour; but the Jews cried out: —

"If thou let this man go, thou art not Cæsar's friend; whosoever maketh himself a king speaketh against Cæsar."[7]

[6] John 19 : 5, 6.   [7] John 19 : 12.

This was touching Pilate in a weak place. He was already under suspicion by the Roman government. He knew that a report of this kind would be his ruin.

"When Pilate saw that he could prevail nothing, but that rather a tumult was made, he took water, and washed his hands before the multitude, saying : —

"I am innocent of the blood of this just person; see ye to it." Caiaphas answered defiantly, "His blood be on us, and on our children."[8]

And the awful words were echoed by the priests and re-echoed by the people.

It was a terrible sentence to pass upon themselves. It was an awful heritage to pass down to their posterity.

Literally was this fulfilled upon themselves in the fearful scenes of the destruction of Jerusalem some forty years later.

Literally has it been fulfilled in the scattered, despised, and oppressed condition of their descendants since that day.

Doubly literal will be the fulfilment when the final accounting shall come. The scene will then be changed, and "this same Jesus" will come "in flaming fire taking vengeance on them that know not God."

Then they will pray to rocks and mountains : —

"Fall on us, and hide us from the face of him that sitteth on the throne, and from the wrath of the Lamb; for the great day of his wrath is come."[9]

[8] Matthew 27 : 24, 25. [9] Revelation 6 : 16.

"Then the soldiers of the governor took Jesus into the common hall, and gathered unto him the whole band of soldiers. And they stripped him, and put on him a scarlet robe.

"And when they had platted a crown of thorns, they put it upon his head, and a reed in his right hand : and they bowed the knee before him, and mocked him, saying, Hail, King of the Jews!

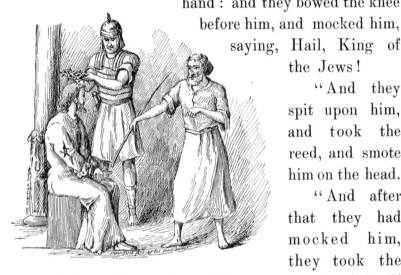

"And they spit upon him, and took the reed, and smote him on the head.

"And after that they had mocked him, they took the robe off from him, and put his own raiment on him."[1]

Satan led the cruel soldiery in their abuse of the Saviour. It was his purpose to provoke him to retaliation, if possible, or to drive him to perform a miracle to release himself, and thus break up the plan of salvation.

One stain upon his human life; one failure of his humanity to bear the terrible test, and the Lamb of

[1] Matt. 27 : 27-31.

God would have been an imperfect offering, and the redemption of man a failure.

But he who could command the heavenly hosts, and in an instant call to his aid legions of holy angels, one of whom could have immediately overpowered that cruel mob,— he who could have stricken down his tormentors by the flashing forth of his divine majesty,— submitted to the coarsest insult and outrage with dignified composure.

As the acts of his torturers degraded them below humanity, into the likeness of Satan, so did the meekness and patience of Jesus exalt him above the level of humanity.

Christ, the precious Son of God, was to be led forth and crucified. Had Pilate acted promptly and firmly at the first, carrying out his own convictions of right, his will would not have been overborne by the mob; they would not have presumed to dictate to him. His wavering and indecision proved his ruin.

How many, like the Roman governor, sacrifice principle and integrity, in order to shun disagreeable consequences. Conscience and duty point one way, and self interest points another; and the current setting strongly in the wrong direction, sweeps away into the thick darkness of guilt him who compromises with evil.

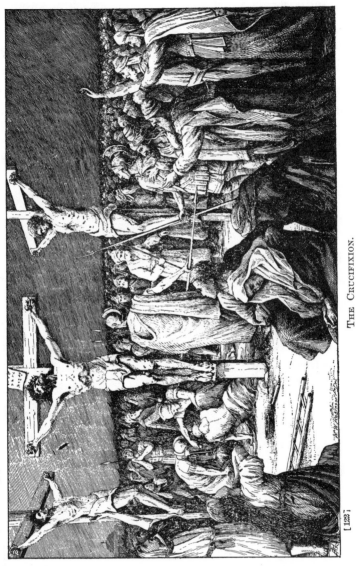

THE CRUCIFIXION.

"If thou be the King of the Jews, save thyself."

Calvary.

JESUS was hurried to Calvary amid the jeers and shouts of the crowd. As he passed the gate of Pilate's court, the heavy cross which had been prepared for Barabbas was laid upon his bruised and bleeding shoulders.

The load was too heavy for the Saviour in his weary, suffering condition. He had gone but a few rods when he fell fainting beneath the cross.

When Jesus revived, the cross was again placed upon his shoulders. He staggered on a few steps, and again fell to the ground as one lifeless. His persecutors now realized that it was impossible for him to go farther with his burden, and were puzzled to find some one who would carry the humiliating load.

Just then they were met by Simon, the Cyrenian, coming from an opposite direction. They at once seized him, and compelled him to carry the cross to Calvary.

The sons of Simon were disciples of Jesus, but he himself had never openly accepted the Saviour. Simon was ever after grateful for the privilege of bearing the cross of the Redeemer. The burden he was thus forced to carry became the means of his conversion. The events of Calvary and the words uttered by Jesus led Simon to accept him as the Son of God.

Arriving at the place of crucifixion, the condemned were bound to the instruments of torture. The two thieves wrestled in the hands of those who stretched them upon the cross; but the Saviour made no resistance.

The mother of Jesus had followed him on that awful journey to Calvary. She longed to minister to him as he sank exhausted under his burden, but she was not allowed this privilege.

At every step of that wearisome way she had looked for him to manifest his God-given power, and release himself from the murderous throng. And now that the final scene was reached, and she saw the thieves bound to the cross, what an agony of suspense she endured!

Would he who gave life to the dead suffer himself to be crucified? Would the Son of God suffer himself to be thus cruelly slain? Must she give up her faith that he was the Messiah?

She saw his hands stretched upon the cross,— those hands that had ever been stretched forth in blessing to the suffering.

The hammer and the nails were brought, and as the spikes were driven through the tender flesh, the heartbroken disciples bore away from the cruel scene the fainting form of the mother of Jesus.

The Saviour made no murmur of complaint; his face remained pale and serene, but great drops of sweat stood upon his brow. His disciples had fled from the dreadful scene. He was treading the wine-

press alone; and of the people there was none with him.[1]

As the soldiers were doing their dreadful work, the mind of Jesus passed from his own sufferings to the terrible retribution that his persecutors must one day meet. His own agony made vivid to his mind the anguish that would be theirs in that day. He pitied them in their ignorance, and prayed : —

[1] Isaiah 63 : 3.

"Father, forgive them; for they know not what they do."[2]

Jesus was earning the right to become the advocate for men in the Father's presence. That prayer of Christ for his enemies embraced the world. It took in every sinner who had lived or should live, from the beginning of the world to the end of time.

As soon as Jesus was nailed to the cross, it was lifted by strong men, and thrust with great violence into the place prepared for it. This caused intense suffering to the Son of God.

Pilate then wrote an inscription in Latin, Greek, and Hebrew, and placed it upon the cross, above the head of Jesus, where all might see it. It read : —

"Jesus of Nazareth the King of the Jews."

The Jews requested that this be changed. Said the chief priests : —

"Write not, The King of the Jews; but that he said, I am King of the Jews."

But Pilate was angry with himself because of his former weakness. He also thoroughly despised the jealous and wicked rulers. So he replied : —

"What I have written I have written."[3]

And now a terrible scene took place. Priests, rulers, and scribes joined with the rabble in mocking and jeering the dying Son of God, saying : —

"If thou be the King of the Jews, save thyself."[4]

2 Luke 23 : 34.   3 John 19 : 19, 21, 22.   4 Luke 23 : 37.

" He saved others; himself he cannot save. If he be the King of Israel, let him now come down from the cross, and we will believe him. He trusted in God; let him deliver him now, if he will have him; for he said, I am the Son of God."[5]

" And they that passed by railed on him, wagging their heads, and saying, Ah, thou that destroyest the temple, and buildest it in three days, save thyself, and come down from the cross."[6]

The unfeeling soldiers divided the clothing of Jesus among themselves. One garment was woven without seam, and a contention arose about it. They finally settled the matter by casting lots for it. This scene had been accurately described by the pen of inspiration : —

" For dogs have compassed me; the assembly of the wicked have inclosed me; they pierced my hands and my feet. . . . They part my garments among them, and cast lots upon my vesture."[7]

[5] Matthew 27 : 42, 43.　　[6] Mark 15 : 29, 30.　　[7] Psalms 22 : 16-18.

DARKNESS ON CALVARY.

"No eye could pierce the gloom surrounding the cross."

Death of Christ.

IT was not the fear of death, nor the pain of the cross, that made Christ's sufferings so terrible. It was the crushing weight of the sins of the world, and a sense of separation from his Father's love, that broke his heart and brought death so soon to the Son of God. Christ felt much as sinners will feel when they awake to realize the burden of their guilt, and that they have forever separated themselves from the joy and peace of heaven.

Angels beheld with amazement the agony of despair borne by the Saviour. His anguish of mind was so intense that the pain of the cross was hardly felt by him.

Nature itself was in sympathy with the scene. The sun shone clearly until midday, when suddenly it seemed to be blotted out. All about the cross it became dark as the blackest midnight. This supernatural darkness lasted fully three hours.

No eye could pierce the gloom surrounding the cross. A nameless terror took possession of all present. The cursing and reviling ceased. Men, women, and children fell upon the earth in abject terror.

Lightnings occasionally flashed forth from the cloud, and revealed the cross and the crucified Redeemer. All thought their time of retribution had come.

At the ninth hour the darkness lifted from the people, but still wrapped the Saviour as with a mantle. The lightnings seemed to be hurled at him as he hung upon the cross. It was then that he sent up the despairing cry : —

"My God, my God, why hast thou forsaken me ?"[1]

In the meantime, the darkness had settled over Jerusalem and the plains of Judea. As all eyes were turned in the direction of the fated city, they saw the fierce lightnings of God's wrath directed toward it.

Suddenly the gloom was lifted from the cross, and in clear, trumpet-like tones, that seemed to resound through creation, Jesus cried : —

"It is finished."[2] "Father, into thy hands I commend my spirit."[3]

A light encircled the cross, and the face of the Saviour shone with a glory like unto the sun. He then bowed his head upon his breast, and died.

The multitude about the cross stood paralyzed, and with bated breath gazed upon the Saviour. Again darkness settled upon the earth, and a hoarse rumbling like heavy thunder was heard. This was accompanied by a violent earthquake.

[1] Mark 15 : 34.   [2] John 19 : 30.   [3] Luke 23 : 46.

The people were shaken into heaps by the earthquake. The wildest confusion and terror ensued. In the surrounding mountains, rocks were rent asunder, and many of them came tumbling down into the plains below. Sepulchers were broken open, and many of the

"The vail of the temple was rent in twain."

dead were cast out of the tombs.

Creation seemed to be breaking into atoms. Priests, rulers, soldiers, and people were mute with terror, and lying prostrate on the ground.

At the time of the death of Christ, some of the priests were ministering in the temple at Jerusalem. They felt the shock of the earthquake, and at the same moment the vail of the temple, which separated the holy from the most holy place, was rent in twain

9

from top to bottom by the same bloodless hand that wrote the words of doom upon the walls of Belshazzar's palace.

The most holy place of the earthly sanctuary was no longer sacred. Never would the presence of God again overshadow that mercy-seat. Never would the acceptance or displeasure of God again be manifested by the light or shadow in the precious stones in the breastplate of the high priest.

From henceforth the blood of the offerings in the temple was of no value. The Lamb of God, in dying, had become the sacrifice for the sins of the world.

When Christ died upon the cross of Calvary, the new and living way was thrown open to Jew and Gentile alike.

Angels rejoiced as the Saviour cried, "It is finished!" The great plan of redemption was to be carried out. The sons of Adam might, through a life of obedience, be exalted finally to the presence of God.

Satan was defeated, and knew that his kingdom was lost.

In Joseph's Tomb.

REASON against the Roman government was the crime for which the Saviour was condemned. Persons put to death for this cause were consigned to a burying ground especially provided for such criminals.

John shuddered at the thought of having the body of his beloved Master handled by the rough and unfeeling soldiers, and buried in a dishonored grave. But he saw no way to prevent it, as he had no influence with Pilate.

At this trying time, Joseph and Nicodemus came to the help of the disciples. Both of these men were members of the Sanhedrim, and were acquainted with Pilate. Both were men of wealth and influence. They were determined that the body of the Saviour should have an honorable burial.

Joseph went boldly to Pilate, and begged from him the body of Jesus. Pilate, after ascertaining that Christ was really dead, granted Joseph's request.

While Joseph was securing the body of the Redeemer from Pilate, Nicodemus brought a costly mixture of myrrh and aloes, of about one hundred pounds' weight, for the burial of the Saviour.

The Burial

The most honored in all Jerusalem could not have been shown more respect in death. The humble followers of Jesus were astonished to see these wealthy rulers taking such an interest in the burial of their Master.

The disciples were overwhelmed with sorrow at the events that had taken place. They forgot that Jesus had told them that just such things were to happen. They were without hope.

Neither Joseph nor Nicodemus had openly accepted the Saviour while he was living. But they had listened to his teachings, and had watched closely every step of his ministry. Although the disciples had forgotten the Saviour's words foretelling his death, Joseph and Nicodemus remembered them well. And the scenes connected with the death of Jesus, which disheartened the disciples and shook their faith, only proved to these rulers that he was the true Messiah, and led them to take their stand firmly for the Saviour.

The help of these rich and honored men was greatly needed at this time. They could do for their dead Master what it was impossible for the poor disciples to do.

Gently and reverently they removed with their own hands the body of the Son of God from the cross. Their tears of sympathy fell fast, as they looked upon his bruised and torn form.

Joseph owned a new tomb, hewn from stone. He had built it for his own use; but he now prepared it for Jesus. The body, together with the spices brought by Nicodemus, was wrapped in a linen sheet, and the Redeemer was borne to the tomb.

Although the Jewish rulers had succeeded in putting to death the Son of God, they could not rest easy. They well knew of the mighty power of Jesus.

They had stood by the grave of Lazarus, and seen the dead brought back to life and glorious manhood, and they trembled for fear that Christ would himself rise from the dead and again appear before them.

They had heard Jesus say to the multitude that he had power to lay down his life and to take it up again.

They remembered that he

Sealing the Tomb.

had said, "Destroy this temple, and in three days I will raise it up."[1]

Judas had told them the words spoken by Jesus to his disciples on their last journey to Jerusalem:—

"Behold, we go up to Jerusalem; and the Son of man shall be betrayed unto the chief priests and unto the scribes, and they shall condemn him to death, and

[1] John 2:19.

shall deliver him to the Gentiles to mock, and to scourge, and to crucify him : and the third day he shall rise again." [2]

They now remembered many things spoken by Jesus which foretold his resurrection. They could not shut out these thoughts, however much they desired to do so. Like their father, the devil, they believed and trembled.

Everything proclaimed to them that Jesus was the Son of God. They could not sleep, for they were more troubled about Jesus in death than they had been during his life.

Desiring to make all things as secure as possible, they requested Pilate to make sure the sepulcher until the third day. Pilate placed a band of soldiers at the command of the priests, and said : —

"Ye have a watch ; go your way, make it as sure as ye can. So they went, and made the sepulcher sure, sealing the stone, and setting a watch." [3]

[2] Matthew 20 : 18, 19.　　　[3] Matthew 27 : 65, 66.

THE HEAVENLY MESSENGER.

"He parts the darkness from his track, and the whole heavens are lighted with his dazzling glory."

"He Is Risen."

Guarding the tomb.

THE greatest care had been taken to guard the tomb of the Saviour, and a great stone had been rolled to its mouth. The Roman seal had been placed upon this stone, so that it could not be moved without breaking the seal.

A well equipped guard of Roman soldiers surrounded the sepulcher. It was their duty to keep strict watch over the tomb, and see that the body which it contained was not molested. Sentinels were constantly pacing to and fro, while the remainder of the detachment took what rest they could.

But there was another guard surrounding that tomb. It was composed of mighty angels from the courts of heaven. Any one of this angel guard, by putting forth his power, could have stricken down the whole Roman army.

The night of the first day of the week has worn slowly away, and the darkest hour, just before daybreak, has come.

One of the most powerful angels is sent from heaven. His countenance is like lightning, and his garments white as snow. He parts the darkness from his track, and the whole heavens are lighted with his dazzling glory.

The sleeping soldiers start to their feet in a body. They gaze with awe and wonder at the open heavens, and the vision of brightness which is nearing them.

The earth trembles and heaves as that powerful being from another world approaches. He is coming on a joyful errand, and the speed and power of his flight shake the world like a mighty earthquake. Soldiers, officers, and sentinels, fall as dead men to the earth.

There had been yet another guard about that burial place. This guard was composed of evil angels. The Son of God had fallen in death, and was even then claimed as the lawful prey of him who hath the power of death,—the devil.

The angels of Satan were present to see that no power should take Jesus from their grasp. But as the mighty being sent from the throne of God approached, they fled in terror from the scene.

One of the commanding angels who had, with his heavenly company, been keeping watch over the tomb of his Master, joined the powerful angel who had just come from heaven. Together they advanced to the sepulcher.

The angelic commander laid hold of the great stone at the mouth of the tomb, rolled it away, and sat upon it. His companion entered the sepulcher and removed the wrappings from the face and head of Jesus. Then, with a voice that caused the earth to tremble, he called forth : —

" Jesus, thou Son of God, thy Father calls thee ! "

Then he who had earned the power over death came forth from the tomb with the tread of a conqueror. As he arose from the dead, the earth reeled, the lightning flashed, and the thunder rolled.

An earthquake marked the hour when Christ laid down his life. Another earthquake witnessed the moment when he took it up again in triumph.

Satan was bitterly angry that his angels had fled at the approach of the heavenly messenger. He had dared to hope that Jesus would not take up his life again ; but his courage failed him as he saw the Saviour come forth from the tomb in triumph. Satan now knew that his kingdom would have an end, and that he must finally die.

Go Tell My Disciples.

LUKE, in his account of the burial of the Saviour, when speaking of the women who were with him at his crucifixion says : —

" And they returned, and prepared spices and ointments ; and rested the Sabbath day, according to the command-ment." [1]

The Saviour was buried on Friday, the sixth day of the week. They prepared spices and ointments with which to embalm their Lord, and laid them aside, until the Sabbath was past.

" And when the Sabbath was past, . . . very early in the morning, the first day of the week, they came unto the sepulcher at the rising of the sun." [2]

As they neared the garden, they were surprised to see the heavens beautifully lighted up, and to feel the earth trembling beneath their feet. They hastened to the sepulcher, and were still more astonished to find

[1] Luke 23 : 56.　　　　　[2] Mark 16 : 1, 2.

that the stone was rolled away, and that the Roman guard was not there.

They noticed a light shining about the tomb, and looking in, saw that it was empty. While Mary was carrying the news to the disciples, the other women examined the sepulcher more closely.

Suddenly they beheld a beautiful young man, clothed in shining garments, and they were afraid. It was the angel who had rolled away the stone, and he said to them : —

"Fear not ye ; for I know that ye seek Jesus, which was crucified. He is not here : for he is risen, as he said. Come, see the place where the Lord lay.

"And go quickly, and tell his disciples that he is risen from the dead ; and, behold, he goeth before you into Galilee ; there shall ye see him ; lo, I have told you." [3]

As the women looked again into the sepulcher, they saw another shining angel, who inquired of them : —

"Why seek ye the living among the dead ? He is not here, but is risen ; remember how he spake unto you when he was yet in Galilee, saying, The Son of man must be delivered into the hands of sinful men, and be crucified, and the third day rise again." [4]

The angels then explained the death and resurrection of Christ. They called the attention of the women to the words that Christ had spoken to them,

[3] Matthew 28 : 5–7.   [4] Luke 24 : 5–7.

in which he had told them beforehand of his crucifixion and of his resurrection. These words of Jesus were now plain to them, and they gathered from them fresh hope and courage.

Mary had been absent during this scene, but now returned with Peter and John. When the rest returned to Jerusalem, she remained at the tomb. She could not bear to leave until she should learn what had become of the body of her Lord. As she stood weeping, she heard a voice which asked : —

"Woman, why weepest thou? whom seekest thou?"

Her eyes were so blinded by tears that she did not observe who it was that spoke to her. She thought it might be one who had charge of the garden, and so addressed him pleadingly : —

"Sir, if thou have borne him hence, tell me where thou hast laid him, and I will take him away."

She thought that if this rich man's tomb was considered too honorable a place for her Lord, she would herself provide a place for him. But now the voice of Jesus himself fell upon her astonished ears. He said to her : —

"Mary."

Her tears were instantly brushed away, and she beheld Jesus. Forgetting, in her joy, that he had been crucified, she stretched forth her hands to him, saying : —

"Rabboni" (Master)!

Jesus then said, "Touch me not; for I am not yet ascended to my Father; but go to my brethren, and say unto them, I ascend unto my Father, and your Father; and to my God, and your God."[5]

Jesus refused to receive the homage of his followers until he should know that his sacrifice had been accepted by the Father. He wished to receive the assurance from God himself that his atonement for the sins of men had been full enough so that through his blood they might gain eternal life.

Jesus immediately ascended to heaven and presented himself before the throne of God, showing the marks of cruelty upon his brow, his hands, and his feet.

But he refused to receive the coronet of glory and the royal robe, as he had refused the homage of Mary, until the Father should signify that his offering was accepted.

[5] John 20 : 13–16.

He also had a request to prefer concerning his chosen ones upon earth. He wished to have the relation clearly defined that his redeemed should hereafter sustain to heaven and to his Father.

His church must be justified and accepted before he could accept heavenly honor. He declared it to be his will that where he was, there his church should be. If he was to have glory, his people must share it with him. Those who should suffer with him on earth must finally reign with him in his kingdom.

In the clearest manner Christ pleaded for his church, identifying his interest with theirs, and advocating, with a love and constancy stronger than death, their rights and titles gained through him. God's answer to this appeal went forth in the proclamation : —

"Let all the angels of God worship him."

Every angelic commander obeyed the royal mandate, and, "Worthy, worthy is the Lamb that was slain; and that lives again a triumphant conqueror!" echoed and re-echoed through all heaven. The innumerable company of angels prostrated themselves before the Redeemer.

The request of Christ was granted — the church is justified through him, its representative and head. Thus the Father ratified the contract with his Son, that he would be reconciled to repentant and obedient men, and take them into divine favor through the merits of Christ.

Witnesses.

LATE in the afternoon of the day of the resurrection, two of the disciples were on the way to Emmaus, a little town eight miles from Jerusalem.

They were perplexed over the events that had recently taken place, and especially concerning the reports of the women who had seen the angels, and had met Jesus after his resurrection.

They were now returning to their home to meditate and pray, in hope of gaining some light in regard to those matters which were so dark to them.

As they journeyed, a stranger came up behind them and joined their company; but they were so busy with their conversation that they scarcely noticed his presence.

These strong men were so burdened with grief that they wept as they traveled along. Christ's pitying heart of love saw here a sorrow which he could relieve.

Jesus, disguised as a stranger, entered into conversation with them. "But their eyes were holden

10

JOURNEY TO EMMAUS.

"What manner of communications are these that ye have one to another,
as ye walk, and are sad?"

that they should not know him. And he said unto them : —

"What manner of communications are these that ye have one to another, as ye walk, and are sad?

"And the one of them, whose name was Cleopas, answering said unto him : —

"Art thou only a stranger in Jerusalem, and hast not known the things which are come to pass there in these days?

"And he said unto them, What things?

"And they said unto him, Concerning Jesus of Nazareth, which was a prophet mighty in deed and word before God and all the people."[1]

They then told the circumstances which had occurred, and related the report of the women who had been at the sepulcher early that same morning. "Then he said unto them : —

"O fools, and slow of heart to believe all that the prophets have spoken : Ought not Christ to have suffered these things, and to enter into his glory?

"And beginning at Moses and all the prophets, he expounded unto them in all the Scriptures the things concerning himself."[2]

The disciples were silent from amazement and delight. They did not venture to ask the stranger who he was. They listened intently as he opened to their understanding the mission of Christ in its completeness.

[1] Luke 24 : 16–19.　　　　[2] Luke 24 : 25–27.

As the sun was setting, the disciples reached their home. Jesus "made as though he would have gone further." But the disciples could not bear to part from their companion who had brought them such joy and hope.

And " they constrained him, saying, Abide with us; for it is toward evening, and the day is far spent. And he

"PEACE BE UNTO YOU."

went in to tarry with them." [3]

The simple evening meal was soon ready, and Jesus took his place at the head of the table, as his custom was.

It was usually the duty of the head of the family to ask a blessing upon the food ; but Jesus placed his hands upon the bread and blessed it. And the eyes of the disciples were opened.

[3] Luke 24 : 28, 29.

The act of blessing the food, the sound of the now familiar voice, the prints of the nails in his hands, all proclaimed him their beloved Master.

For a moment they sat spellbound; then they arose to fall at his feet and worship him; but he suddenly disappeared from their midst. They forgot their hunger and weariness. They left the meal untasted, and hastened back to Jerusalem to bear to the others the precious message of a risen Saviour.

As they were relating these things to the disciples, Jesus himself stood among them, and, with hands uplifted in blessing, said : —

"Peace be unto you." [4]

At first they were frightened; but when he had shown them the prints of the nails in his hands and feet, and had eaten before them, they believed and were comforted. Faith and joy now took the place of unbelief, and they acknowledged their risen Saviour with feelings which no words could express.

Thomas was not with them at this meeting. He refused to believe the reports in regard to the resurrection. But after eight days Jesus appeared to the disciples again when Thomas was present.

On this occasion Jesus showed the signs of his death in his hands and feet. Thomas was at once convinced, and cried : —

"My Lord and my God." [5]

[4] Luke 24 : 36.

[5] John 20 : 28.

THE ASCENSION.

"With hands outstretched in blessing, he slowly ascended from among them."

[152]

This Same Jesus.

This same Jesus shall so come in like manner....

THE work of the Saviour on earth was finished. The time had now come for him to return to his heavenly home. He had overcome, and was again about to take his place by the side of his Father upon his throne of light and glory.

Jesus selected the Mount of Olives as the place of his ascension. Accompanied by the eleven, he made his way to the mountain. But the disciples were not aware that this was their last season with the Master. As they walked, the Saviour gave them their last instructions. Just before leaving them, he made that precious promise so dear to every follower of Jesus: —

"Lo, I am with you alway, even unto the end of the world."[1]

They crossed the summit, to the vicinity of Bethany. Here they paused and gathered about their Lord.

[1] Matthew 28 : 20.

Beams of light seemed to radiate from his countenance as he looked with love upon them. Words of the deepest tenderness were the last which fell upon their ears from the lips of the Saviour.

With hands outstretched in blessing, he slowly ascended from among them. As he passed upward, the awestruck disciples looked with straining eyes for the last glimpse of their ascending Lord. A cloud of glory received him out of their sight. At the same moment there floated down to them the sweetest and most joyous music from the angel choir.

While the disciples were still gazing upward, voices addressed them which sounded like richest music. They turned, and saw two angels in the form of men, who spoke to them, saying : —

" Ye men of Galilee, why stand ye gazing up into heaven ? this same Jesus, which is taken up from you into heaven, shall so come in like manner as ye have seen him go into heaven." [2]

These angels belonged to the company that had come to escort the Saviour on his way to his heavenly home. In sympathy and love for those left below, they had stayed to assure them that this separation would not be forever.

Jesus had promised to come again, for he said : —

" Let not your heart be troubled ; ye believe in God, believe also in me. In my Father's house are many mansions ; if it were not so, I would have told

[2] Acts 1 : 11.

you. I go to prepare a place for you. And if I go and prepare a place for you, I will come again, and receive you unto myself; that where I am, there ye may be also." [3]

The angels declared to the disciples that Jesus will "so come in like manner as ye have seen him go into heaven." He ascended bodily, and they saw him as he left them and was received by the cloud. He will return on a great white cloud, and "every eye shall see him."

Enoch testified, "Behold, the Lord cometh with ten thousand of his saints, to execute judgment upon all." [4]

Isaiah prophesied that the righteous will proclaim at his coming, "Lo, this is our God; we have waited for him, and he will save us."

Paul, describing the same scene, said : —

"For the Lord himself shall descend from heaven with a shout, with the voice of the archangel, and with the trump of God; and the dead in Christ shall rise first:

"Then we which are alive and remain shall be caught up together with them in the clouds, to meet the Lord in the air; and so shall we ever be with the Lord." [5]

Thus will our Saviour come to earth to take to himself forever those who have been loyal to him.

[3] John 14 : 1–3.   [4] Jude 14.   [5] 1 Thessalonians 4 : 16, 17.

Their Ascended Lord.

"Then returned they unto Jerusalem from the mount called Olivet."

WHEN the disciples returned to Jerusalem alone, the people expected to see in their faces expressions of sorrow and defeat. Instead of this, they beheld only gladness and triumph.

The disciples did not mourn over disappointed hopes, but were constantly in the temple, praising God. The priests and rulers were at a loss to understand this mystery.

After the trial and crucifixion of their Master, it was expected that the disciples would appear defeated and ashamed. But they came forth joyously, their faces aglow with a happiness not of earth.

They told the wonderful story of the glorious resurrection of Christ and his ascension to heaven, and many believed their testimony. They had no longer any distrust of the future.

They knew that Jesus was in heaven; that his sympathies were still with them; that he was plead-

ing with God the merits of his blood. He was showing to the Father his wounded hands and feet, as an
evidence of the price he had paid for his redeemed.

They knew that he would come again, with all
the holy angels with him,
and they looked for this
event with great joy and
longing anticipation.

"Lift up your heads, O ye
gates, and the King of Glory
shall come in."

When he passed from their
sight on the Mount of
Olives, he was met by a
heavenly host, who, with songs of joy and triumph,
escorted him upward.

At the portals of the city of God an innumerable
company of angels await his coming. As they approach the gates, the angels who are escorting the
Saviour, in triumphant tones address the company at
the portals : —

> "Lift up your heads, O ye gates;
> And be ye lift up, ye everlasting doors;
> And the King of glory shall come in."

The waiting angels at the gates inquire : —
> "Who is this King of glory?"

The escorting angels reply in songs of triumph : —
> "The Lord, strong and mighty,
> The Lord, mighty in battle.
> Lift up your heads, O ye gates;
> Even lift them up, ye everlasting doors;
> And the King of glory shall come in."

Again the waiting angels ask : —
> "Who is this King of glory?"

The escorting angels reply in melodious strains : —
> "The Lord of hosts,
> He is the King of glory." [1]

Then the portals of the city of God are opened wide, and the angelic throng sweep through the gates amid a burst of rapturous music. All the heavenly host surround their returned Commander as he takes his place upon the throne of the Father.

With adoration and joy, the angels bow before him, while the glad shout fills all the courts of heaven : —

" Worthy is the Lamb that was slain to receive power, and riches, and wisdom, and strength, and honor, and glory, and blessing." [2]

The Son of God has triumphed over the prince of darkness, and conquered death and the grave. Heaven rings with voices in lofty strains proclaiming : —

" Blessing, and honor, and glory, and power, be unto him that sitteth upon the throne, and unto the Lamb for ever and ever." [3]

[1] Psalms 24 : 7-10.   [2] Revelation 5 : 12.   [3] Revelation 5 : 13.

*"And one shall say unto him,
what are these wounds in thine hands?
Then he shall answer, Those with
which I was wounded in the house
of my friends."*
Zechariah 13:6 (KJV)

*"Greater love hath no man
than this, that a man lay down
his life for his friends."*
John 15:13 (KJV)

If you have enjoyed this book on the life of Christ for young readers, may we recommend "The Desire of Ages" by the same author for older readers. This book is considered by many to be the most in-depth "spiritual" biography on the life of Christ ever written. A leading curator of the library of congress acclaimed the contents poignant and outstanding. This book is the end of any true seekers search for personal hope, comfort and happiness.

862 pages, Cloth, $14.95